Edexcel
Success through qualifications

BTEC
NATIONAL

> **Award**

> **Certificate**

> **Diploma**

SPORT

John
Honeybourne

Published in 2003 by:
Nelson Thornes Ltd
Delta Place
27 Bath Road
CHELTENHAM
GL53 7TH
United Kingdom

03 04 05 06 07 / 10 9 8 7 6 5 4 3 2 1

A catalogue record for this book is available from the British Library

ISBN 0 7487 7100 X

Illustrations by Angela Lumley and Oxford Designers and Illustrators
Page make-up by Florence Production Ltd
Index by Indexing Specialists (UK) Ltd

Printed and bound in Italy by Canale

Contents

Introduction

This book is designed for students and their teachers, covering the theoretical requirements for many of the more popular units in the BTEC Sport and BTEC Sport and Exercise Science qualifications. Whether students are studying for the Award, the Certificate or the Diploma level of qualification, they will find the material in this book extremely beneficial. The book gives information in a form that is easily accessible to students, and is one of many important sources from which students can draw in this fascinating and exciting area of study. A list of references and further reading, and a glossary of the key terms, which will help students to support the basic knowledge acquired through this book, is included.

The BTEC qualifications are growing in popularity, and enable teachers and students to concentrate on topics that can be related to sport. There are many theoretical concepts that can be applied to sport, including physiological, psychological and sociological components. This book addresses these main academic disciplines and applies theoretical principles and issues to practical sports situations. The start of each chapter lists clear learning objectives that identify the areas of study to be covered.

The BTEC qualifications are delivered by teachers in a variety of ways, including direct teaching, guided learning, group work, practical work and problem solving. This textbook will help teachers to deliver the course using these approaches.

Assessment of BTEC qualifications includes completion of assignments and external tests; using this book students will be able to prepare for the written tasks, and in revising for external tests. Many practical examples and definitions will help to clarify the subject matter and become useful points for reference when writing assignments.

At the end of each chapter are questions designed to check students' progress; these can form the basis of tasks leading to assignment completion, or can be used as useful revision points for external tests.

Acknowledgements

I would like to thank my wife Rebecca and the rest of my family for being so supportive while I was writing this book.

The authors and publishers would also like to thank the following people for permission to reproduce material:

- *The Times*, London (22 September 2002), for Table 5.4 on calorie expenditure.
- Hodder & Stoughton Educational for Tables 5.1, 5.2, 7.2 and 7.3 taken from Wesson, K. *et al.* (2000) *Sport and PE*, pp. 141–142, 711, and for Figure 6.1 taken from Woods, B. (1998) *Applying Psychology to Sport*.

Every attempt has been made to contact copyright holders, and we apologise if any have been overlooked. Should copyright have been unwittingly infringed in this book, the owners should contact the publishers, who will make corrections at reprint.

Photo credits

- Peter Adams/Digital Vision BP (NT) – Figure 2.10 (p.24)
- Corbis UY (NT) – Figure 10.7 (p.141)
- Corel 174 (NT) – Figure 6.23 (p.103)
- Corel 329 (NT) – Figure 2.9 (p.24)
- Corel 423 (NT) – Figure 2.6 (p.22)
- Corel 778 (NT) – Figure 2.13 (p.27)
- Digital Vision XA (NT) – Figure 2.5 (p.22)
- Getty Images (UK) Ltd – Figures 1.1 (p.2), 1.2 (p.2), 1.6 (p.5), 1.7 (p.6), 1.8 (p.7), 1.9 (p.8), 1.10 (p.9), 1.13 (p.12), 1.14 (p.14), 1.15 (p.15), 1.16 (p.16), 1.17 (p.17), 2.1 (p.19), 2.2 (p.20), 2.3 (p.20), 2.8 (p.24), 2.11 (p.25), 3.6 (p.37), 4.4 (p.43), 4.10 (p.49), 4.30 (p.56), 5.6 (p.74), 5.7 (p.75), 6.2 (p.86), 6.3 (p.88), 6.4 (p.89), 6.5 (p.90), 6.6 (p.91), 6.7 (p.92), 6.8 (p.92), 6.9 (p.93), 6.10 (p.94), 6.11 (p.95), 6.12 (p.95), 6.13 (p.97), 6.14 (p.97), 6.15 (p.98), 6.18 (p.100), 6.19 (p.101), 6.20 (p.101), 6.21 (p.102), 6.22 (p.102), 7.2 (p.107), 7.3 (p.108), 7.4 (p.108), 7.5 (p.110), 7.6 (p.110), 7.7 (p.111), 7.9 (p.114), 7.11 (p.116), 8.1 (p.119), 8.2 (p.120), 8.3 (p.121), 8.4 (p.123), 8.5 (p.124), 10.1 (p.137), 10.2 (p.138), 10.3 (p.138), 10.4 (p.139), 10.5 (p.140), 10.9 (p.141), 10.11 (p.143), 10.12 (p.143), 10.13 (p.144), 10.14 (p.145), 10.16 (p.148), 10.17 (p.149), 11.1 (p.153), 11.2 (p.154)
- Instant Art (NT) – Figures 3.2 (p.36), 3.3 (p.36) and 3.4 (p.36)
- Photodisc 18 (NT) – Figure 4.29 (p.55)
- Photodisc 61 (NT) – Figure 10.6 (p.140)
- Photodisc 67 (NT) – Figure 5.3 (p.71).

1

Sport in society

This chapter is designed to deal with the theoretical elements of this core unit and investigates the issues that relate to sport and society. To understand the issues that affect sport today, it is important to have a cultural perspective, and the chapter gives an overview of this area. The way in which sport is organised and social factors both affect participation and performance in sport, and these influences are covered in detail here.

Learning objectives

- To outline the organisation of sport in the UK.
- To review the development and changing nature of sport.
- To identify funding sources in sport.
- To review the role of the media in sport.
- To identify and explain the social influences on sport participation.
- To explore the scale of the sport industry.
- To examine the role of local, national and European agencies in sport.

1.1 Organisation of sport in the UK

The organisations that are associated with sport in the UK are **public**, **private** and **voluntary**. The taxpayer (via the government) funds the public organisations. Private-sector organisations include commercial businesses trying to make a profit and non-profit-making voluntary organisations such as the Youth Hostels Association or amateur sports clubs.

A detailed description of local, national and European agencies will be given later in this chapter.

⫴ *In practice*

If you want to become fit you can use public, private or voluntary facilities and equipment to exercise. Public facilities include the local leisure centre, run by the local authority and funded by taxpayers. Better or more convenient facilities may be provided by the private sector – such as a private health and fitness club. Voluntary-sector organisations include your local athletic club, where you could turn up on club night to train with people of similar fitness levels. If you wish to keep fit by walking or rambling, then you might join the Youth Hostels Association, another voluntary organisation, which would give you information and concessionary rates to stay at youth hostels.

1.2 The development of sport

Historically sport has had a major influence on our society, by preparing the populace for war, to hunt for food or to improve their fitness to work.

In medieval times, the peasants had little time or energy to be involved in activities that were nothing to do with working on the land. However, activities like mob football – which brought together the whole village on holy days and festivals – did take place.

The activities of the ruling classes eventually became the sports that we know today. For instance, hunting was an exclusive activity for the upper classes because they had the land and the money. They also had more time on their hands, which was not the case for the lowly peasants.

In the nineteenth century the upper classes began to send their children to schools called public schools. Although the word 'public' suggests that everyone was involved, the schools were exclusive to the upper classes – and, to start with, for boys only. In these public schools the sporting activities that were popular became the forerunners of the sports that we know today, with rules, facilities and organised ways of playing.

After the middle of the nineteenth century, sport really started to develop quickly. One major factor that influenced the development and participation in sport was the amount of leisure time available.

Figure 1.1 Mob games at public schools

Figure 1.2 Rowing developed as a sport in public schools

Increased leisure time

Before the **industrial revolution** most of the work was on the land and there was no real distinction between work and leisure. Agricultural work was dictated by the seasons and there was no set 'free' time for the workers. With the development of industry working hours were long and pay was poor. A 72-hour working week was not uncommon for a worker at that time, and workers therefore had very little time and energy for sport. The **Saturday half day** was very important in sports development, providing a short period of time to play sport. Skilled workers were given this halfday before the manual labourers but by the late nineteenth century most workers had more time for sport and leisure. However, even given the extra time the workers did not have much taste for active sport because of their poor working and living conditions (there was a great deal of deprivation and poverty at that time), but sports clubs did start to develop. The factory owners recognised that a happier, more contented workforce would be more effective and encouraged the development of these clubs.

In the larger factories the owners would also pay for an annual excursion for their workers, such as a trip to the seaside. This was the beginning of the seaside holiday.

Figure 1.3

By 1965, a working week of 40–45 hours was typical, but today the average working week is about 37 hours. This makes it much easier to be involved in sport. By law, workers should have at least four weeks' holiday a year, which again makes it easier for people to participate in and watch sport.

Public transport and car ownership

Historically there was little transport available for the vast majority of the population. Before the twentieth century transport was restricted mainly to walking and horseback. There were of course river communications and eventually canals, but it was the development of roads, the bicycle, the

Figure 1.4

railways and eventually the motor car that enabled good communication and travel. The railways in particular were very important in the development of seaside resorts, and allowed sports fixtures to be played (and spectators to be able to visit) in venues all round the country.

Cars began to be mass-produced in the twentieth century and now most households own a car. This means that spectators can easily follow their sports teams around the country, and participation in sport is also easier because transport is so much more readily available than 50 years ago.

Role of physical education in schools

Sport has also developed as a result of what has happened in school physical education. Physical education lessons encourage the development of skills that are used in many sports, and a great number of extracurricular sports activities are organised. Examination courses in physical education have raised the awareness of the role of sport in society and there are many links between schools and local sports clubs and other recreation providers.

The **National Curriculum** is a list of courses the government considers that all state schools (from primary schools to the age of 16 in secondary schools) must deliver, and one of the stated aims of the National Curriculum is to get as many children as possible to participate actively in sport.

Physical education also involves the learning of information related to health, fitness and diet.

Over the last 20 years physical education has been affected by a huge growth in facilities such as new sports centres and all-weather playing surfaces. There has also been a recent initiative – schools are becoming specialist sports colleges.

Sports colleges

The sports colleges initiative is only one part of the Specialist Schools Programme introduced by the government (other specialist colleges teach performing arts, technology and modern foreign languages, for instance).

Figure 1.5 There has been a large growth in the leisure industry over the last 20 years

The programme is designed to give a distinctive identity to a school. Schools must develop partnerships with other schools, the local community and with private-sector sponsors. The government gives additional funding for such specialist colleges to develop their specialism.

The objectives of the sports colleges initiative are to:

- extend the range of opportunities available to children
- raise the standards of teaching and learning of PE and sport
- develop the school's identity
- benefit other schools in the area, including primary and secondary schools
- strengthen the links between schools and private sponsors
- increase participation in PE and sport for students both under and over 16 years and to develop the potential of talented performers.

At the time of writing, sports colleges attract additional funding of a one-off grant of £100 000 and an extra £120 per pupil per year for four years. So not only do schools benefit by raising awareness of PE and sport, but they are also financially rewarded – which is why many schools are seeking to become sports colleges. The Youth Sports Trust (YST) is responsible for the validation of a sports college. There is more information on the Youth Sports Trust later in this chapter.

National training organisations

With the growth of the leisure and recreation industry over the last 20 years, there has been a need for the industry to ensure high standards of training. In 1995 SPRITO, the sport and recreation industries training organisation, was launched.

1.3 Recent changes in participation in sports

- The number of local authority-run sports facilities available has increased and the quality has improved.
- There has been an explosion of privately run health and fitness clubs and the leisure and recreation industry is one of the most important in the UK.
- A larger cross-section of people take advantage of sports facilities and more and more people are regular participants in sport.
- Health and fitness activities are now 'fashionable' and being fit and looking good is an important aspect of our culture.
- The average life expectancy of the population has increased and there are more and more older people who can take advantage of sports opportunities. There are more veterans' teams in a variety of sports and there is a growing awareness that activity in old age can enrich the quality of life.
- People with disabilities now have much better access to sport. Disability sport is recognised as a sport in its own right, and UK participants have achieved great success in international competition.

Definition

SPRITO

This is the national training organisation for sport, recreation and allied occupations. It includes training for leisure attractions, health and fitness, the outdoors, the caravan industry, playwork and sport and recreation.

Figure 1.6 More and more older people can take advantage of sports opportunities

Figure 1.7

- The media have also played a part in changing the nature of sport in the UK. The increase in technology brings sporting events from around the world live into our living rooms every day. Sport is often headline news, with documentaries, films and promotion of products that are associated with sport. These all raise the profile of sport and feed the interest and enthusiasm for sport. We will cover the influence of the media in more detail later in the chapter.

1.4 Income and funding developments in sport

The influence of sponsorship on the development of sport has been enormous. Sport is now big business, with commercial companies spending large amounts of money on sports' participants and events. For example, a large company such as Adidas might sponsor a top-class tennis player to wear a particular style of training shoe. At the other end of the scale, a local hockey club may attract a small amount of money to go towards the first-team kit.

There has also been a significant increase in sponsorship as sports clothing has become fashionable. For instance, there has been a huge increase in sales of training shoes – many people wear 'trainers' who would never dream of participating in sport! Nevertheless commercial companies recognise that top sports stars can be fashion role models and therefore use

Figure 1.8 Sport is big business

them in advertising campaigns. For example, Eric Cantona and many other top football stars were featured heavily in an advertising campaign during the 2002 World Cup.

1.5 The influence of the media on the development of sport

The media influence sport and sport influences the media. Both need each other. Television companies in particular have spent a great deal of money to obtain the broadcasting rights to sports events. Increasingly, subscribers to some channels must pay extra to view certain events (such as boxing) – this is often called pay-per-view. For example, Sky holds the rights to many Premiership football games, which you can only view if you subscribe to a Sky package. Digital TV has also influenced sport – but not always to anyone's benefit. The collapse of ITV Digital in 2002 meant that many football clubs faced financial disaster, because they had been promised large sums of money that they did not receive.

The terrestrial channels such as BBC and ITV have lost the rights to show many of the major sports events and there have been ludicrous examples of the BBC news being unable to show a clip of a boxing match, for instance, because the rights to that match are owned by another company. Never before has there been so much coverage of sport on TV but, because of satellite TV dominating this coverage, only those who can afford to subscribe have access to many sports events.

The type of sport that gets the most coverage is limited, with football getting the most. Male sport also still dominates, although there is a refreshing interest in women's football, for instance.

The rules of sport have been influenced by the media and event programming has been revised because of the needs of the TV companies. For example, football fans are finding that their team may play on a Sunday at 6.00 p.m. – not traditionally a timeslot for the game; Olympic events are often scheduled at unsuitable times because of the demands of TV companies, who are beaming the event across different time zones. Even rules have been affected due to the influence of TV. For instance, in cricket the 'third umpire' – in the form of a video replay analysis – has been introduced. There has been a similar development in rugby football. The armchair spectator can now see the event from every angle and the officials' decisions are laid bare for scrutiny, hence new technology is needed to aid the decision-makers on the field.

The extent of media involvement has also influenced the amount of sponsorship and advertising revenue available to participants, clubs and sports organisations. This has brought much-welcomed money into sport, but some argue that this has only been to a small number of participants in a small number of sports and may well have led to the decrease in participation in minority sports.

The media can increase participation in sport – you only have to see the increased activity on municipal tennis courts during the Wimbledon fortnight to appreciate that watching sport can stimulate participation. Interest in playing a sport is particularly increased when the media highlight the success of UK performers. For instance, there was a surge of interest in curling after our success in the Winter Olympics.

Figure 1.9 TV has a big influence on sport

▍*In practice*

Types of media involved in sport:
- *Television – BBC, ITV, Channel 4, Channel 5, satellite, cable, digital, factual/fiction/advertising.*
- *Press – broadsheets, tabloids, local, weekly, magazines, periodicals.*
- *Radio – national, local, commercial.*
- *Cinema – documentaries, movies (USA/UK/Bollywood, etc.).*

1.6 Social influences on sport participation

There are many factors that encourage or discourage participation in sport. Your culture is an important influence. Some cultures do not encourage women to participate in sport; in some cultures sport is a high-status activity, in others it is not valued.

There is still a difference in the participation levels of men and women in sport, and there is a long tradition of discrimination against women in sport. Women were discouraged in the nineteenth and early twentieth centuries because it was thought to be dangerous to their health and childbearing potential. Some people still think that being good at or interested in sport is unfeminine, thus reinforcing male dominance in sport and sports coverage. Even now the media often cover women's sport because of their appearance rather than their achievements. For instance, in women's tennis there is a huge discrepancy in prize money, with women getting far less than men. The media show a lot of interest in tennis players such as Anna Kournikova because of their looks, but at the time of writing Anna

Figure 1.10 More women are now getting recognised in sport

has achieved little on the international circuit. She has a highly lucrative deal with a bra manufacturer, even though she has had relatively little success.

However, there are many positive aspects of women in sport. More women are now involved in physical exercise than ever before; there is far more interest in health and fitness matters; women now play sports such as football and rugby and are getting at least some recognition. There is an increase in female sports presenters, which may encourage more women to take an interest in sport, and there are fewer instances of open discrimination against women participating in clubs such as golf clubs.

Other social influences on sport participation include race, social class, economic status and disability. The problems with 'access' need to be solved for each group if there is to be widening of participation in sport.

Reasons for participation and non-participation

Time

Many people decide not to participate in sport because of work commitments. It is common to hear the phrase 'I haven't got the time'. However, the perception of how much time is available is often very different from reality. For example getting home from work and watching television all evening is a way of spending your leisure time, and shows that there is leisure time. Some people choose to spend what leisure time they have in a passive rather than active way.

Resources

Depending on where you live there may or may not be sports facilities or clubs nearby. This has an obvious effect on whether you participate in sport or not. One way of increasing participation would be a transport service readily available for those who wish to visit a sports facility.

Figure 1.11 Don't be a 'couch potato'!

Definition

Learned helplessness

This is a psychological phenomenon that arises from failure on a task or tasks that has been reinforced. There is then avoidance behaviour with that task or tasks. 'I was hopeless at sport at school, it is no good me trying sport again – I will only fail.'

Fitness/ability

Some people do not join in sports activities because they think that they are not good enough. This perception may well have arisen from previous experiences, e.g. failing in an activity at school, feeling humiliated by it and therefore feeling that they are a hopeless case. In psychology we call this feeling 'learned helplessness'.

To get rid of this feeling of hopelessness, it is important that individuals experience success in some aspect of sport so that they regain their confidence. After all it is extremely unlikely that there is *no* sport that you cannot be even remotely good at!

▌▌▌*In practice*

'Sport is getting youngsters away from crime and helping fight drug abuse.'
(verdicts from reports commissioned by Sport England in 2002).

In Bristol, there has been a 40% reduction of crime levels on the Southmead Estate since the first sport development worker was appointed.

Health problems

There are genuine health reasons for some people not to participate in sport, although many medical practitioners will encourage an active lifestyle as much as possible. Most rehabilitation regimes include physical exercise, and what better way to exercise than playing sport? The amount of obesity in the western world has increased due to our diet and lack of exercise.

Embarrassment is a powerful emotion that prevents many people taking the step towards sport. For such people to be involved in sport they need to be encouraged and the right environment provided. Joining clubs such as 'Weight Watchers' can encourage some people to take exercise, which may lead to participation in a sport, but some people say that joining such an organisation is demeaning and only reinforces lack of self-worth. Lack of self-esteem is an important factor and must be tackled for an individual to gain the confidence necessary to participate in sport.

Access

The growth of sports facilities has increased access but, although more low-cost courses are available, some people still cannot afford to participate in sport. For many the most important questions that influence access, are: What is available? What is affordable? How do I feel about myself? This is sometimes identified in the three words: **provision**; **opportunity**; **esteem**.

The main issues related to access are:

- **Opening times** – e.g. may not be convenient for shift workers.
- **Age** – e.g. sport is often perceived as a young person's activity and elderly people may feel undignified if they participate in sport.
- **Race** – e.g. racial discrimination may reduce a person's confidence in getting involved in a predominantly white environment such as a golf club.
- **Class** – e.g. polo is often played by people from the upper middle classes. It is perceived to be a 'posh' person's sport.
- **Disability** – e.g. lack of suitable facilities such as wheelchair ramps or wide enough doors for disabled people to take part.

In practice

In Luton, the participant's ethnic origin is a huge influence on the types of sports chosen. For example, just 2% of Pakistani residents go swimming, compared with 36% of white and Indian people.

(from The Player – Sport England summer 2002)

In practice

People on low incomes living in a disadvantaged community in the north of England demonstrate some of the lowest levels of participation in sport ever measured.

(headline from The Player – Sport England summer 2002)

- *Of people from social groups D and E 70% take part in at least one sport but in Liverpool this figure is only 51%.*
- *In Bradford the proportion of children swimming, cycling or walking is less than half the national average.*
- *43% of British children play cricket, but in Liverpool only 3% do.*
- *However, in these areas the vast majority of children have a very positive view about the value of sport.*

Issues in sport

To encourage more people to participate in sport the government, schools, sports clubs and local authorities have produced a number of initiatives.

Schools

The growth of specialist sports colleges is designed to increase participation, but the government (via the National Curriculum) and physical education teachers are working hard at making sport as accessible as possible. Extracurricular activities, the use of sports awards and the use of external coaches and agencies are all designed to increase participation.

III In practice

In October 1998 the Education and Standards Framework Act was passed. Section 77 states that every decision on the disposal of a school playing field has to be taken by the Education Secretary. Before that it was estimated that more than 5000 playing fields had been sold off, regardless of the purpose of the sale. The Act made it law that the proceeds of any sale were to be invested in sports or educational provision.

Child protection

There has been much in the press about children being at risk of abuse by sports coaches. This is, thankfully, still very rare but steps have been taken to ensure that all those who work with children are cleared by the Criminal Records Bureau. The organisation sports coach UK (formerly known as the National Coaching Foundation) is also compiling a register of responsible coaches.

The Children Act 1989 has had a big impact on people who work with children. Although the age range of the Children Act was up to eight, the legislation has affected the provision for all school-aged children. The United Nations Convention on the Rights of the Child, especially Articles 12 and 31, has also changed the way in which workers view children. These articles encourage us to view children as a 'rightful stakeholder', rather than a 'needy minor'.

1.7 Scale of the sports industry

The sports industry has grown rapidly since 1990. A massive amount of money has been invested in sport and sports-related goods and services. Sport today is heavily commercialised, with worldwide potential. Widespread TV coverage has enabled businesses to promote their products across the globe.

Sponsorship is an important part of sport, with many sponsors spending millions of pounds to have their brand name or logo emblazoned on an athlete's shirt.

III In practice

During the Commonwealth Games in Manchester in 2002, the display of advertising logos and names was not allowed. This instruction was curiously ignored when David Beckham played a part in the opening ceremony. The fact that he is also a professional football player, rather than a sportsman associated with the Commonwealth Games, also illustrates the power of big business.

Figure 1.13 Sport today is heavily commercialised

Sport in the UK is of great economic importance. Private health clubs estimate that in 1999, the health club market was worth £2.25 billion. Sports participation expenditure in 1998 was £2.3 billion. There has been a significant shift over the last 30 years from the UK being a manufacturing economy to a service economy, with an explosion in the leisure industry.

In practice

Football League clubs are turning to gambling to stave off bankruptcy. Up to 20 clubs are in talks with gaming operators about opening casinos in their grounds.

(The Guardian, 9 June, 2002)

Sport-related employment has also risen significantly – over half a million people now work in jobs related to sport. This is more than the people employed in the chemical, agricultural and coal industries.

There is a growing business in health and fitness clubs and more recently personal trainers have become fashionable – and not just for the very rich. In many health and fitness clubs, personal trainers give a personal information and motivation service to people who want to train in the right way and have someone to push them to achieve more.

There is an increase in employment opportunities in the sports and leisure industry, for example, coaches, trainers, administrative staff, physiotherapists, massage specialists, leisure centre managers, entertainers, grounds maintenance, corporate hospitality managers and workers.

There is also a huge growth in the sports manufacturing industry, largely due to sportswear being so fashionable.

1.8 Structures and role of local, national and European agencies

Department for Culture, Media and Sport (DCMS)

This is a government department that has responsibility for government policy related to sport. This department decides what is provided and what is spent using taxpayers' money. In the year 2000/1, the budget for the department was approximately £1 billion, 90% of which goes directly to service providers in cultural and sporting sectors.

The budget is forecast to be approximately £1.6 billion by 2005/6, including £25 million for coaching, £6 million for talent scholarship, £20 million per year for facilities at community amateur sports clubs and a guarantee on maintaining levels of funding through the World Class Performance Programme. For more information go to the website: www.culture.gov.uk.

UK Sport

In 1972, the national sports councils were formed and were deemed to be independent from the government. In 1996, there was a reorganisation of the sports councils and UK Sport, or the UK Sports Council was formed.

The role of UK Sport is as an agency under government direction, to provide support for elite sportspeople who have a high level of performance or have the potential to reach the top. The organisation not only distributes government funds, including Lottery money, but also supports world-class performers and promotes ethical standards of behaviour, including the fight against the use of performance-enhancing drugs through its anti-doping programme.

UK Sport delivers its services through six directorates:

- Performance Services
- International Relations
- Major Events
- UK Sports Institute
- Corporate Services
- Anti-doping.

UK Sport oversees the work of each home-country sports council. These are:

- Sport England
- Sportscotland
- Sports Council for Northern Ireland
- Sports Council for Wales.

More information can be found from info@uksport.gov.uk.

Figure 1.14 The Commonwealth Games in Manchester (2002)

UK Sports Institute (UKSI)

The aim of this organisation is to provide the very best sportspeople with appropriate facilities and support. It provides sports science advice, coaching expertise and top training facilities. The UKSI comprises a number of centres located around the UK. Each individual home-country sports council has responsibility for the development of the UKSI in its area.

More information can be found from uksi@uksport.gov.

Figure 1.15 The UKSI provides the very best facilities and support

sports coach UK (scUK)

This organisation used to be called the National Coaching Foundation. Its brief is to guide the development and implementation of a coaching system for all coaches in the UK. Activities include:

- running coaching courses
- administering coaching qualifications
- providing coaching resources
- working with governing bodies to raise the quality of coaching schemes
- producing a national register of coaches to ensure an ethical and secure coaching structure, especially concerning child protection.

For more information look at www.sportscoachuk.org.

Youth Sports Trust (YST)

The YST has created a sporting pathway for all children through a series of linked schemes called the TOP programmes. It is a sports agency responsible for the development of sport for young people. It is a registered charity and was established in 1994. The YST has developed schemes to encourage young people from 18 months to 18 years to take part in sport and to follow a healthy and active lifestyle.

Governing bodies

Most of the sports that we know today were developed and organised in the late nineteenth century. The participants needed to agree rules and regulations for their sports and so they met and formed their own committees called governing bodies (examples are the FA, LTA, ASA and RFU). There are over 265 governing bodies in the UK.

Teams and clubs pay a subscription to their sport's governing body, which administers the sport nationally and organises competitions and the national team. There are still many amateur positions within each governing body, but increasingly more salaried staff are involved.

The national governing bodies are also members of international governing bodies such as UEFA and FIFA. These international bodies control and organise international competitions.

Central Council of Physical Recreation (CCPR)

This is the 'umbrella' organisation for the national governing and representative bodies of sport and recreation in the UK. Its aim is to promote, protect and develop the interests of sport and physical recreation. This organisation is completely independent from government control and has no responsibility for allocating funds.

Figure 1.16 Sports tournaments, such as Wimbledon, have high organisational demands

The European Non-Governmental Sports Organisation (ENGSO)

ENGSO is an increasingly effective organisation that represents the views of sports bodies throughout Europe and works towards raising the status of sport in Europe.

European Parliament Sports Inter Group

There is no legal basis for sport in the Treaty of Rome and therefore sport has little status in the European Parliament. This organisation provides a forum for MEPs to meet to discuss factors affecting sport in Europe.

The European Social Fund (ESF)

This is an important source of funding for activities to develop employability and human resources. The ESF provides up to 45% of the costs of a project. 'Matched funding' is then obtained from other sources. One of the most important objectives of the ESF is to improve economically disadvantaged areas and areas adjusting to changes in their industrial and service sectors. This is an important source of funding for projects on sports-related employment in the UK.

British Olympic Association (BOA)

The BOA was formed in 1905. Great Britain is one of only five countries that has never failed to be represented at the Olympics since they began in 1896. The BOA supplies the delegates for the National Olympic Committee (NOC), which is responsible amongst other things for the planning and execution of the Great Britain Olympic Team's participation in the Olympic and Winter Olympic Games.

More information can be found on www.olympics.org.uk.

International Olympic Committee (IOC)

The IOC was created by the Paris Congress in 1894. It owns all the rights to the Olympic symbol and the Games themselves. This is the world body that

Figure 1.17 The IOC administers the Olympic Movement

administers the Olympic Movement. Its headquarters are in Lausanne, Switzerland. Members are appointed to the IOC and are responsible for selecting the host cities of the Olympic Games, both summer and winter.

Progress check

1 Define what is meant by public, private and voluntary organisations in sport. Give an example of an organisation in each group.
2 What are the characteristics of 'mob football'?
3 Why was the introduction of the Saturday half day so important in the development of sport?
4 Describe the links between transport and sports development.
5 What are the main objectives of the sports colleges initiative?
6 What is the role of SPRITO?
7 Describe some of the recent changes in sports participation.
8 How can the media influence sport?
9 What are the reasons for the lower sports participation rates of women?
10 Explain some of the reasons for non-participation in sport.
11 Describe the structures and roles of the following organisations:
   (a) UK Sport
   (b) The UK Sports Institute
   (c) The Youth Sports Trust.

2

Ethics and values in sport

This chapter is designed to encourage an understanding of the standards, ethics and values associated with sport. Sport is often viewed as an important contributor to the personal development of individuals, and at the highest level involves a large amount of physical and emotional commitment. This chapter will look at the roles, responsibility and behaviour expected from and associated with professional sportspeople, employers, amateurs/volunteers, performers and spectators. The key principles of responsibility and good practice will be dealt with so that ethical codes can be applied to sports coaching, performance, training and instruction.

Learning objectives

- To investigate and identify the principles, values and ethics associated with sport.

- To recognise the application of values and ethics in a range of sports situations.

- To give relevant information for a code of practice to be drawn up for use in sport.

- To enable a sport's activity to be planned using appropriate principles, ethics and values.

2.1 Principles, values and ethics

A principle is a basic truth, law or policy. **Principles** are standards that define moral behaviour. A principle in sport might be that the officials treat all equally on the field of play. **Values** are ideals that form the basis of actions and beliefs. Values in sport include enjoyment, quality of movement, fitness and health, and character building. **Ethics** are rules that dictate your conduct. They form a system of rules that groups and societies are judged on. An ethic in sport would be that you stick to the spirit of the rules of the game.

In practice

Principles, values and ethics in sport:

- **Principles** – *Sport must be played fairly without discrimination by officials. For example, the referee in a rugby match is expected to make decisions on what has happened on the field of play, regardless of who the player is. This illustrates the principle of fair play in sport. In Premier League football teams it is often thought that England players 'get away' with behaviour that would be deemed unacceptable and against the principle of fair play.*

Figure 2.1 Sport must be played fairly without discrimination by officials

- **Values** – *A player should endeavour to play well for the team's sake and not for his or her own benefit. For example, a hockey goalkeeper would put herself at some risk by saving a hard-driven shot – this upholds the value of playing for the sake of others. In Premier League football a goalkeeper may try very hard to save a shot and risk injury because he is due to gain as an individual in a forthcoming transfer deal. This is not upholding the value of playing for others.*

Figure 2.2 A player should endeavour to play well for the team's sake

Figure 2.3 In sport it is ethical to acknowledge that you have broken the rules

- **Ethics** – *In sport it is ethical to acknowledge that you have broken the rules of your particular game. For example, a snooker player would tell the referee that he had committed a foul shot even though the referee had not noticed – this shows ethical conduct. In athletics, a runner might take a performance-enhancing drug, breaking the rules of competition – this is an example of unethical behaviour.*

Case study

After six weeks of deliberation, in October 2002 the Court of Arbitration for Sport (CAS) decided to confirm the International Olympic Committee's (IOC) decision to disqualify Alain Baxter from the men's alpine skiing slalom event at the Salt Lake City Winter Games.

Baxter finished third in the slalom and was awarded the bronze medal, but a subsequent doping test revealed traces of methamphetamine in his urine sample – a stimulant on the IOC's list of prohibited substances.

Although Baxter maintained that the US Vicks nasal inhaler he used before the slalom race contained levmetamphetamine – a non-performance-enhancing isomer of methamphetamine – the CAS ruled that the anti-doping code of the Olympic movement prohibits all forms of methamphetamine and the presence of any prohibited substance results in automatic disqualification, whether or not ingestion was intentional.

'The panel is not without sympathy for Mr Baxter, who appears to be a sincere and honest man who did not intend to obtain a competitive advantage in the race,' the tribunal concluded.

'I'm gutted not to be getting my medal back but there's a lot of positive things to come out of this,' said Baxter. 'I also feel it's not just my loss. I'm getting things back as normal and in future maybe the policies will change a little bit.'

Baxter now falls under the British Olympic Association's doping by-law, which states that any athlete found guilty of a doping offence is ineligible to represent Great Britain at any future Olympic Games. An athlete can appeal against the by-law, however, on the basis that there were significant mitigating circumstances and/or the offence was minor.

'Alain has paid a most severe penalty for a modest mistake and it is clear that the principle of strict liability under-scored this decision,' added Simon Clegg, Chief Executive of the BOA. 'I know that I can continue to look Alain in the eye with confidence that he did not knowingly take the US Vicks inhaler to enhance his performance.'

Adapted from a report in the UK Sport Newsletter 2002.

Consider the principles, values and ethics involved in the above description.

The National Training Organisation (NTO) states that every individual in the sports and recreation field, whether paid or unpaid, should:

- aim to be competent in their role – measured against national standards
- be able to become qualified for recognition of competence
- have access to appropriate training
- have a professional development programme to maintain competence.

The UK Coaching Review has a vision that reads:

> *By 2012 the practice of coaching in the UK will be elevated to a profession acknowledged as central to the development of sport and the fulfilment of individual potential.*
>
> *For the above to be realised coaching must have:*
> - *professional and ethical values and inclusive and equitable practice*
> - *agreed national standards of competence*
> - *regulated and licensed profession*
> - *appropriate funding*
> - *culture of professional development.*

Figure 2.4 Coaching is central to the development of sport

The NTO and other organisations related to sport and recreation recognise the importance of suitable ethical standards that include equality of opportunity and inclusiveness – in other words, no one should be discriminated against within the industry.

In practice

The National Occupational Standards Level 2

The following key assumptions underpin the coaching process and will help coaching to have its intended impact on participants.

1. *The participant must be at the centre of the process. When coaching, the coach should support, co-ordinate and manage the process effectively, always starting with the identification and recognition of the participant's needs, and should aim to address those needs through their coaching.*

2. *Coaches should empower participants, supporting their right to make choices, discover their own solutions, and enabling them to participate and develop at their own pace and in their own way.*

3. *Coaches should provide opportunities and an environment that motivates, controls risk, engenders challenge, enjoyment and – above all – achievement.*

4. *Coaches should aim to grow participants' confidence and self-esteem.*

Coaching is fundamentally about providing a safe and ethical environment in which participants are able to maximise their potential within a sport or activity. For participants to achieve their maximum potential, they must learn in an environment that is safe, supportive and free from distractions. This will be achieved by the coach providing the right equipment, having good working relationships with all those involved, maintaining their health, safety and welfare, and controlling the behaviour of participants and other people involved in the session.

Figure 2.5 Coaches should provide opportunities to motivate and control risks!

Figure 2.6 Coaches should empower participants

2.2 Value statements

NVQs in sport and recreation and allied occupations have the value statement that **there should be no prejudice based on**:

- disability
- social and economic disadvantage
- race
- gender
- age.

Figure 2.7 There should be no prejudice based on age

The value statement emphasises the importance of:

- being flexible to meet participants' needs
- assisting individuals to make the right choices and decisions
- supporting participants to make choices and decisions
- supporting participants to achieve and exercise self-determination
- extending participants' knowledge beyond their immediate experience
- building confidence and individuality
- valuing diversity
- providing a stimulating environment that gives opportunities for enjoyment, risk, challenge and achievement
- encouraging the growth of confidence and self-esteem
- ensuring physical and personal safety.

▌▌▌*In practice*

Sport England's Equity Statement
'Sport England recognises that inequalities in sport exist. We are working to change the culture and structure of sport to ensure that it becomes equally accessible to all.'

Figure 2.8

Some facts should be taken into account when assessing whether sport is inclusive and lacks discrimination:

- 40% of children in London are of ethnic origin.
- Women in social group AB are 44% more likely to participate in sport than women in social group DE.
- 72% of people in social group ABC1 use local-authority sports facilities, compared with 50% of the population as a whole.
- Of young people with a disability 13% were members of a sports club in 1999 (compared with 46% of non-disabled young people).
- 20% of elite performers attended private schools, but only 6% of the population did.

Figure 2.9 Is sport totally inclusive?

2.3 Equity legislation

Detailed guidance and codes of practice are available from the Equal Opportunities Commission (www.eoc.org.uk). Other useful sources of information are the Disability Rights Commission (www.drc-gb.org.uk) and the Commission for Racial Equality (www.cre.gov.uk).

The main anti-discrimination laws in the UK are:

Figure 2.10 There have been important laws passed relating to equal opportunities

- Race Relations Amendment Act 2001 (Race Relations Act 2000). This makes it unlawful to discriminate directly or indirectly on the grounds of colour, race, nationality, ethnic or national origin.
- Human Rights Act 1998.
- Sex Discrimination Act 1986. This makes it unlawful to discriminate directly or indirectly on the grounds of a person's sex or marital status.

⫼ *In practice*
Discrimination as a result of selection for sports on basis of nationality, place of birth or length of residence are exempted.

▮▮▮ *In practice*

The Sex Discrimination Act

Section 29 states that private sports clubs are exempt from provisions of the Act and many complaints are recorded about discrimination against women in private golf clubs (e.g. having no voting rights on club policies).

Section 34 allows for the establishment of single-sex sports clubs.

Section 44 allows any sport to be restricted to one sex where the strength and stamina of the average woman would put her at a disadvantage to the average man.

Figure 2.11 There have been many complaints recorded against women in private golf clubs

- Disability Discrimination Act 1995. This makes it unlawful for an employer of 15 or more staff to discriminate against current or prospective employees on the grounds of disability.
- Special Educational Needs (SEN) and Disability Act 2001.
- Rehabilitation of Offenders Act 1974.
- Employment Protection (Consolidation) Act 1978.

▮▮▮ *In practice*

Private sports clubs are exempted from the Disability Discrimination Act.

2.4 Principles and ethics for staff employed in sports facilities

Staff in sports facilities includes managers, general staff, coaches and trainers. There are a number of principles that underpin the ethical rules in such facilities.

The following are examples of the standards expected for good practice for coaches and trainers:

- Give the participants and other people appropriate time and attention.
- Help all people feel welcome and at ease.
- Communicate with people using the most effective methods, providing the information they need.
- Encourage participants to ask questions when they need to.
- Listen to, and take account of, what people have to say.
- Handle any disagreements in a way that will allow the session to continue and achieve its objectives.
- Make sure your relationships with participants are supportive and in line with accepted good practice and relevant codes of practice.
- Provide everyone involved in the session with clear information on the rules for behaviour and the reasons for these rules.
- Encourage and reinforce behaviour that helps participants work well together and achieve the session's goals.

- Identify and respond to any behaviour likely to cause emotional distress or disruption to the session in a way that is in line with accepted good practice.
- Manage the participants' behaviour effectively and fairly, in a way appropriate to their needs.

2.5 General principles

Staff employed in sports facilities should follow these general principles:
- Treat people with dignity.
- Build respectful relationships with others.
- Take responsibility over your own actions and act responsibly.
- Be committed to the aims of the organisation and to the principles that are held by that organisation.
- Be co-operative with others and show high standards of integrity (which includes confidentiality where appropriate).
- Do not abuse any privileges assigned to you.
- Maintain high standards of personal behaviour and honour the trust given by clients, employers, colleagues and the general public.
- Use a high degree of sportsmanship where appropriate.
- Follow the law.
- Be particularly careful of health and safety issues.
- Minimise any impact on the environment (e.g. clear up litter).

Figure 2.12 Build respectful relationships with others

2.5 Child protection

With thousands of children taking part in sports each week, safety is a priority. Every adult involved in sport – coaches, referees, adult helpers and club members – must be aware of child-protection issues. The National Society for the Prevention of Cruelty of Children (NSPCC) and Sport

England set up their Child Protection in Sport Unit to assist people working with children in sport in implementing child protection policies and helping to ensure that all sporting activity, at whatever level, is safe.

In practice

'Keeping Children Safe in Sport': NSPCC Child Protection Awareness Programme

'Keeping Children Safe in Sport' has been designed to help sports organisations deal appropriately with child protection issues. It will help clubs safeguard the children in their care by enabling staff and volunteers to recognise and understand their role in child protection.

The key benefits outlined by the NSPCC are:
- *You will gain an understanding of child protection issues.*
- *You will be able to recognise signs that a child needs help.*
- *You will feel more confident to take that first vital step to get assistance.*
- *You can demonstrate to others that you have completed a formal programme on child protection awareness.*
- *You will be making an important contribution to preventing children suffering from child abuse.*
- *You will receive a certificate of completeness from the NSPCC.*

Sports coach UK workshops

To support coaches working with children sports coach UK offers a range of resources:
- *Safe and Sound* (introductory leaflet).
- *Good Practice and Child Protection* (workshop for sports coaches).
- *Protecting Children* (home study pack).

Figure 2.13

2.6 Impact of principles and ethics

Individuals and organisations need to assess the impact of their actions and beliefs on:

- management
- employees
- participants
- attitudes of all who are associated with the organisation
- customer satisfaction
- participation rates
- revenue
- standing in local community.

The ways in which the impact can be assessed include questionnaires, interviews, staff turnover and audits of data – for example, counting how many people are using the facility and ascertaining the most popular activities.

Progress check

1 Give one example of a principle, a value and an ethic that relates to sport.
2 Give two value standards that are related to NVQs in Sport and Recreation.
3 List two facts that show discrimination in sport.
4 Explain why the examples of discrimination you listed in Question 3 exist.
5 What can be done to limit discrimination in sport?
6 Describe the content of the following Acts of Parliament:
   (a) Disability Discrimination Act (1995)
   (b) Human Rights Act (1998)
   (c) The Sex Discrimination Act (1986).
7 Give an example in sport where there is exemption from at least one of the Acts listed in Question 6.
8 Describe some of the standards related to ethics that are expected from staff employed in sports facilities.
9 (a) Why is child protection such an issue?
   (b) What is the NSPCC highlighting in its guidance to sports clubs?
10 How can we assess the impact of our actions and beliefs on sports organisations?

3

Health and safety

This chapter covers the necessary aspects of health and safety introduced in the BTEC specifications that apply health and safety to the working environment related to sport. The legislation involved and its impact on staff, clients and sports participants will be examined. The responsibilities held by employers and employees in providing a healthy and safe environment are highlighted.

Learning objectives

- To identify the key legislation and important regulations applicable to sport.

- To investigate how an organisation manages and promotes health and safety.

- To give information that will form the basis of risk assessments for a variety of hazards within sport.

- To explore the benefits to an organisation of effectively managing health and safety and security.

3.1 Key legislation and important regulations

It is important that you are able to describe the following acts and regulations and explain the impact of such legislation on sport.

Health and Safety at Work Act (HSWA) (1974)

Staff training had to be radically overhauled to take into account the conditions in the Act. When the Act came into force there were big improvements in the quality of premises and equipment. It also led to better staff working conditions.

The Act includes:

. . . securing the health, safety and welfare of persons at work and for protecting others against risks to health or safety . . . controlling the keeping and use of dangerous substances . . . controlling emissions into the atmosphere . . .

In practice

The HSWA has been called an 'enabling' act – it allows for further regulations without full legislation via parliament. For example, after the tragedy in Lyme Bay in 1993, when four canoeists died during an outing from an outdoor activity centre, a further act came into force – the Activity Centre (Young Persons' Safety) Act (1995).

European Directives (1992)

The European Community passed six laws that relate to health and safety:

Management of Health and Safety at Work Regulations (MHSW)

This concerns how employers and employees manage their facilities so that there are adequate health and safety procedures.

Personal Protective Equipment at Work Regulations (PPE)

This concerns the wearing of appropriate safety equipment such as goggles and ear defenders.

Manual Handling Operations (MHO)

This law means that employers must find ways of making manual handling of equipment less hazardous.

Health and Safety (Display Screen Equipment) Regulations (DSE)

It is now commonplace for workers to work in front of a computer display screen for many hours each day. These regulations are designed to protect such workers by ensuring adequate training, work breaks and a suitable environment.

Workplace (Health and Safety and Welfare) Regulations (HSW)

These regulations are concerned with the working environment and have replaced the Factories Act. Most leisure situations, other than outdoor education, are covered by these regulations.

These regulations state that employers must provide:
- a good working environment
- appropriate facilities (e.g. toilets and rest areas)
- safety of pedestrians and vehicles
- safety of facilities including doors, windows, escalators, etc.

Provision and Use of Work Equipment Regulations (PUWER)

These regulations relate to the maintenance of equipment. They ensure that working conditions are appropriate and users are trained in use of equipment.

Control of Substances Hazardous to Health Regulations (COSSH) (1994)

A hazardous substance is one that is toxic, harmful, corrosive or an irritant. In the leisure and recreation industry there is widespread use of chemicals – for cleaning, hygiene and disinfection. In swimming pools in particular chlorine and ozone are used to keep pool water clean. These regulations concern their storage and use.

Employers must:
- Have a code of practice for the control of hazardous substances.
- Employ a trained risk assessor.
- Inform all staff of regulations and published guidance.
- Make sure that hazardous substances are used only where absolutely necessary.
- Train staff adequately in the use of personal protection and emergency procedures.
- Have a system of maintaining control of hazardous substances – e.g. how long they are to be stored.
- Monitor the handling of hazardous substances.

Working Time Regulations (1998)

These are linked to employment legislation, which is designed to protect workers from exploitation and overwork. If staff work very long hours then there are obviously health and safety issues to be considered. Tired staff will lose concentration and are more likely to make mistakes, which could be very dangerous for themselves and others. Group leaders of outdoor sports activities may have responsibility 24 hours per day for several days.

These regulations state that no worker is obliged to work more than an average of 48 hours per week. If an employee wishes to work longer hours, he or she must sign an opt-out clause. Many of the people employed by the leisure industry work part-time and so these regulations do not apply quite so much as in other industries.

Health and Safety (First Aid) Regulations (1981)

An organisation must have a procedure for treating injuries in place to conform to these regulations. People working in the leisure and recreation industry supervise and participate in activities that have risks associated with them:
- Some people do not follow the rules.
- Participants may have a known (or unknown) existing medical condition.
- There are many chance circumstances that may result in injury.

One of the most important elements of these regulations is that clear and accurate records must be kept of any incidents – including the circumstances and possible causes of the accident. These records are important to help reviews of risk assessments and to prevent similar accidents happening again. In the present climate of increased litigation, it is also very important to keep records in case there are legal proceedings following an accident.

Some serious accidents or outbreaks of disease must be reported to the appropriate authority (such as the local authority's environmental health department) under the Reporting of Injuries, Diseases and Dangerous Occurrences Regulations (1995), also known as **RIDDOR**.

The Children Act (1989)

This had a huge impact on the industry, especially play work. It places a greater emphasis on care provision and child protection. The Children Act was aimed at children under the age of eight, but its interpretation has had an impact on the provision for all school-aged children. There has been a growing demand for trained and qualified play workers, for instance, because of the ratio of fit person to child numbers necessary (8:1 for children under eight). Records must be kept of accidents, attendance and names of all employees and volunteers.

The awareness of the possibility of child abuse has increased and the people working in the sport and leisure industry are often in positions of trust with children. This Act protects not only the children but also the adults working with them who may be accused – falsely or accidentally – of abuse.

In practice

The Children Act – examples of guidance

- *Do not get into isolated situations with children.*
- *Physical contact must be minimal and involve only non-sensitive areas of the body such as the hands.*
- *Use physical restraint only in emergencies.*
- *Show appropriate role-model behaviour – e.g. do not swear, smoke or drink alcohol.*

The Disability Discrimination Act (DDA) (1995)

The DDA covers those who need support to carry out day-to-day activities. It makes it illegal for any business to discriminate against people with disabilities, either for employment or for providing goods and services ('disabilities' include wheelchair use, sensory impairments and learning difficulties). This Act applies only to businesses with 20 or more employees.

There are very few tasks that people with disabilities cannot do if the equipment or task is suitably modified. It is an offence for any organisation to refuse to serve a person because they have a disability. Also, the service provided to people with disability must not be any less than the service given to people without disabilities. Many outdoor activities can create problems for those with disabilities and there are exemptions in the Act to cater for these.

Safety at Sports Grounds Act (1975)

This Act is concerned with large sports stadia that will take at least 10,000 spectators. The Act requires that:

- A stadium can be used only after a safety certificate has been issued.
- This certificate is valid only for the activities stated.
- The number of spectators allowed in the stadium is specified.
- A record of attendance is kept.
- Records of maintenance to the stadium must be kept.

The owners and managers of such stadia are criminally liable if the Act is not implemented so it is a strong and important legislative Act.

This is a very important Act. The behaviour of people in crowds can be erratic and if there is panic people may suffer crush injuries, resulting in death. The number of very large sports stadia in the UK has grown since the beginning of the twentieth century and there was often little control over the numbers of people allowed into each stadium and how the spectators were controlled. Consequently there have been some dreadful disasters:

- At the football Cup Final in 1923 there were many injuries and loss of crowd control.
- Disasters at Bolton Wanderers (1946) and Ibrox stadium (1971) prompted public inquiry.
- Bradford 1986 – fire disaster.
- Hillsborough 1989 – disaster involving many deaths.

These disasters prompted the government to tighten up legislation to make stadia safer.

Fire Safety and Safety of Places of Sport Act (1987)

This expanded the scope of the Safety at Sports Grounds Act. The following are key components:

- Fire and safety certificates have to be issued by the Fire Authority.
- Facilities need to have procedures in place to prevent and control fires and help people escape from fire.
- Grounds that are deemed hazardous by the Fire Authority can be closed.
- The Act applies to all sports grounds, including temporary stands.
- Indoor sports venues are also included in this legislation.

The Taylor Report (1990) recommended that all Football League grounds should be all-seaters and highlighted safety issues. The 'Green Guide', which relates to the requirements of the Act for all sports grounds, gives 76 recommendations – including:

- Defined maximum capacities for terraces that should be stewarded and monitored.
- Use of closed-circuit television.
- Gangways to be kept clear.
- Fences and barriers must be made less hazardous.
- Planned police involvement.
- There must be one first aider per thousand spectators.
- A doctor should be present if there are more than 2000 people in the crowd.

Food Safety Act (1990) and Food Safety (General Food Regulations) Act (1995)

In the sport and leisure industry, food is often prepared and sold. This Act aims at limiting the likelihood of people contracting food poisoning. The Act has enabled other regulations concerning the preparation, handling, processing, manufacturing, storage and distribution of food. Food premises must be clean and well maintained and all employees trained in the handling of food.

The Data Protection Act (1998)

This Act makes it illegal to use information about individuals for any other purpose other than that for which it was given. The information must be kept secure and accessed only by authorised personnel. The control of data on databases should be protected by a password known only by authorised personnel. Sport and leisure organisations often keep computer files containing personal information about their clients, and the security of this information comes under the DPA.

3.2 Management and promotion of health and safety

The management of organisations in the sport and leisure industry (e.g. local authority sports centres, private health clubs, outdoor education centres and voluntary sports clubs) must take into account health and safety legislation. They should provide safety clothing where appropriate, adequate alarm systems and emergency action plans. All facilities and equipment are to be inspected regularly to ensure they are safe to use; this may include employing safety officers.

Training of staff is very important to ensure a safe environment. All organisations must have training policies in position, with a training programme that includes updating of skills and safe practice, ways of reporting and recording incidents and accidents.

The documentation held by the organisation should be regularly reviewed and updated and procedures should be rigorously monitored and evaluated. Promotional material related to health and safety should be displayed in the organisation – for example posters and fact-sheets that deal with health and safety matters.

Sound safety management strategies will not only ensure a safe working environment but will also:

- ensure efficiency and cost-effective operations
- lower insurance premiums
- ensure the organisation has a good reputation
- increase sales/client usage
- ensure the staff are confident and secure.

3.3 Risk assessment

To minimise risks and ensure safe practice in sports and leisure organisations an appropriate risk assessment strategy must be in place.

Here are some facts regarding accidents in sports and leisure facilities:

- Only seven staff fatalities were reported between 1991 and 1997.
- Between 1991 and 1997 only 21 deaths of participants were reported, including four deaths from horse-riding accidents.
- The Royal Society for the Prevention of Accidents (RoSPA) reports that there are over 400 drownings per year, with 5% happening in swimming pools.
- The number of injuries in this sector is growing, mainly due to 'slips and trips'.

There are many possible hazards in sport and leisure – from diving into a swimming pool to tripping over in a football crowd. Risk assessment should be undertaken regularly to prevent accidents happening.

Definition

Risk assessment

The technique by which you measure up the chances of an accident happening, anticipate what the consequences would be and plan what actions are needed to prevent it.

Procedures of risk assessment

Identifying hazards

The area of the activity must be examined and possible hazards identified. People's perceptions of the area should also be ascertained. Facilities and equipment in use often carry warnings of possible injuries and these must be taken into account when doing a risk assessment. The activity, the equipment or the facilities provided may have obvious risks – for example an AstroTurf all-weather surface is notorious for causing friction burns.

It must be remembered that sports activities carry many inherent risks and without those risks sport would be less exciting and perhaps lose its popularity. However, the risks can be minimised with sufficient care and attention to detail. The main causes of injury in sports are:

- objects falling
- trips and falls
- electric shock
- crowds
- poisoning
- being hit by something (e.g. a javelin)
- fire
- explosion
- asphyxiation.

Identifying who might be harmed

Provision must be made for participants who might not be fully aware of obvious risks, for instance children or people with learning difficulties. Once anyone at particular risk is identified, staff should assess *how* they might be harmed and put into place safety procedures to ensure that the risks are minimised.

Evaluating whether existing safety measures are adequate

The danger caused by a particular hazard should be assessed, and the risks associated with that hazard rated as high, moderate or low. If a hazard is particularly dangerous and the risks are high, then clearly the more serious an accident could be.

In many cases it is best to remove the hazard altogether, for instance a barrier that has been erected in an unhelpful position or a broken swing in a children's playground. Some hazards can be modified in some way to lower the risks – for example glass can be replaced by non-breakable plastic.

The risks arising from some hazards can be limited by using protective equipment. For example, a squash player could wear protective goggles to minimise the risk of being hurt by a blow from the ball.

Often a hazard is supervised to minimise the risks – for example, a lifeguard at a swimming pool.

Making a record of your judgements

The risk assessment should be recorded (this is in fact law, if an organisation has five or more employees).

Definition

Hazard

Something that has the potential to cause harm.

Risk

The chance that someone will be harmed by a hazard.

Evaluating and revising the assessment regularly

Assessments often become out of date as soon as they have been completed, so it is important to review all risk assessments regularly. After any incident that causes (or nearly causes) injury, procedures should be reviewed. If any aspect of the risk assessment was not accurate or realistic, a reassessment should be carried out and procedures reviewed and changed if necessary.

3.4 Managing health and safety and security

The enforcing authorities have a right to inspect premises and have the power to close them down if necessary. Inspectors can suggest how improvements could be made and give a timescale for their implementation.

‖‖*In practice*

Examples of enforcing authorities

- *The Health and Safety Executive*
- *Police*
- *Fire service*
- *Environmental Health officers*
- *Coastguard.*

The employers should also carry out regular inspections, either formally or informally. Formal inspections will be scheduled and informal inspections may include the expectation of staff keeping an eye on possible hazards.

It is important that employers take advantage of the advice available to them from safety inspectors (e.g. Fire Officer) and put into action policies that will not fail any future inspection.

It is important for employers to make available as much information as possible to staff and the public so that everyone recognises the risks involved in any activity and the possible ways of minimising them. The use of signs, for instance, is very important in raising awareness of health and safety issues.

Figure 3.1

Figure 3.2

Figure 3.3

Security

Facilities, equipment and people should be safe from attack or damage, including theft. The issue of security is becoming increasingly important: more attacks on staff are being reported in the public-service sector, although they are fortunately still rare. The main threat is theft, which is common in sports and leisure facilities.

Closed-circuit TV (CCTV) is increasingly being used as a deterrent for crime in public places. Staff monitoring CCTV can take action to deal with any incident. CCTV also provides a videotape record that may help to identify criminals. The use of bright lighting and removal of overgrowing shrubbery also help to deter criminal activity.

Sports halls and leisure centres usually provide secure lockers for use by staff and the general public. Clear marking of equipment can also help to trace stolen goods.

There is also a growth in the private security industry. Many organisations will hire security staff to patrol their premises and car parks, which can deter criminals and give employees and participants a sense of well-being.

Figure 3.4 CCTV is increasingly being used as a deterrent

Figure 3.5 Security is now a high priority in sports events

Progress check

1 Why is the Health and Safety at Work Act (1974) relevant to the sport and leisure industry?
2 Identify some substances that could be hazardous in a sports context.
3 List the six European Directives (1992) related to health and safety.
4 What does RIDDOR stand for?
5 Why was the Children Act (1989) passed?
6 Using a football match as an example, explain the health and safety regulations that must be adhered to.
7 What happened in terms of legislation after the Lyme Bay tragedy?
8 Give an example of an organisation that is associated with sports participation and outline some possible health and safety strategies that staff may employ.
9 Why is it so important to record incidents related to health and safety?
10 (a) What is meant by risk assessment?
    (b) What are the main stages of a risk assessment?
11 Give some suggestions about making a leisure centre's premises more secure.

4

The body in action

This chapter will provide information about how the body responds and adapts to exercise. The structure of the skeletal and muscular systems and their role in producing movement related to sport will be covered. Sections on the structure and function of the cardiovascular and respiratory systems are included, and the information necessary for investigating short-term responses and long-term adaptations to exercise given.

Learning objectives

- To identify the structure and function of the skeletal and muscular systems.

- To explore movement analysis in sports activity.

- To identify the structure and function of the cardiovascular and respiratory systems.

- To investigate the short-term and long-term responses and adaptations of the cardiovascular and respiratory systems to exercise.

A sound knowledge of anatomy will help you understand what happens to the body during and after exercise.

4.1 The skeleton

The skeleton has four major functions:
1. To give shape and support to the body – posture.
2. To allow movement of the body by providing sites for muscle attachment and providing a system of levers.
3. To protect the internal organs such as the heart, lungs, spinal cord and brain.
4. To produce blood – red and white blood cells.

The **axial skeleton** is the main source of support and is the central part of the skeleton. It includes the cranium, the vertebral column and the ribcage (twelve pairs of ribs and the sternum).

The **appendicular skeleton** consists of the remaining bones – arms, legs and the girdles that join these bones on to the axial skeleton.

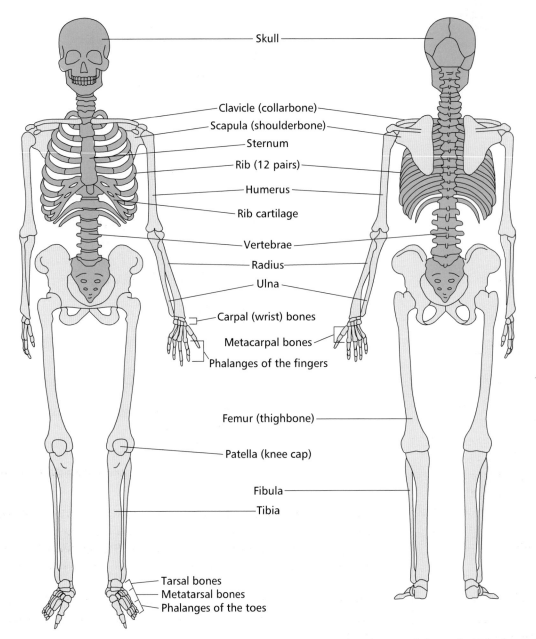

Figure 4.1 A human skeleton showing the major bones

Bones

The bones of the skeleton have designs related to their function. There are several types of bones:

- **Long bones** comprise a hollow shaft of compact bone, which is enlarged at each end consisting of cancellous bone. An example is the tibia.
- **Short bones** are roughly cube-shaped and consist mainly of cancellous bone, which is covered by a thin layer of compact bone. The carpals are short bones.

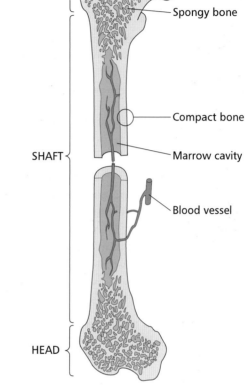

HEAD

— Cartilage

— Spongy bone

— Compact bone

SHAFT

— Marrow cavity

— Blood vessel

HEAD

Figure 4.2 Structure of a long bone

Definition

Compact bone

This hard bone forms the surface layers of all bones. It helps to protect bones and is surrounded by the periosteum, which is a fibrous, vascular tissue containing blood vessels.

Cancellous bone

This is often called **spongy bone** and has a honeycomb appearance, which provides a strong structure that is very light. It consists of bone tissue called **trabeculae**, which is connective tissue, with red bone marrow.

- **Flat bones** protect the internal organs of the body and provide sites for the attachment of muscles. An example is the sternum.
- **Irregular bones** have a variety of shapes with projections. They have a variety of functions, for instance the vertebrae protect the spinal cord.
- **Sesamoid bones** are very specialised, small bones that help with joint movements. They are covered with articular cartilage. The patella is a sesamoid bone.

Cartilage

This is soft connective tissue. Newly born babies have a skeleton with a high amount of cartilage, which is mostly replaced by bone as they get older – a process known as **ossification**. Cartilage has no blood vessels but receives nutrition though diffusion from the surrounding capillary network.

There are three basic types of cartilage:
- **Yellow elastic cartilage** is flexible tissue (e.g. part of the ear lobe).
- **Hyaline** or **blue articular cartilage** is found on the articulating surfaces of bones. It protects and allows movement between bones with limited friction. Hyaline cartilage thickens as a result of exercise.

- **White fibrocartilage** consists of tough tissue that acts as a shock absorber. It is found in parts of the body where there is a great amount of stress, for example the semilunar cartilage in the knee joint.

Joints

There are many different types of joint in the human body, including some that allow very little, or no, movement. Joints are very important in movements related to sport. Joints may be roughly divided into three types:

- **Fibrous** or **fixed joints** do not allow any movement. Tough, fibrous tissue lies between the ends of the bones. Examples are the sutures of the cranium.
- **Cartilaginous** or **slightly moveable** joints allow some movement. The ends of the bones are covered in tough fibrous cartilage, which absorbs shocks and gives stability. The intervertebral discs in the spine are cartilaginous joints.
- **Synovial** or **freely moveable** joints are the most common joints in the body. They allow a wide range of movement so these joints are very important to sports participants. A synovial joint consists of a joint capsule lined with a synovial membrane. The joint is lubricated by synovial fluid. This is secreted into the joint by the synovial membrane. The knee joint is a typical synovial joint.

Types of synovial joint

- **Hinge joint** – allows movement in one plane only (uniaxial). Example: the knee joint.

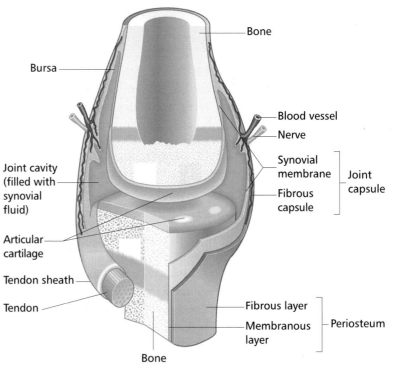

Figure 4.3 A synovial joint

Figure 4.4 The shoulder joint allows a wide range of movement

- **Pivot joint** – allows rotation only and is therefore also uniaxial. Example: axis and atlas of the cervical vertebrae.
- **Ellipsoid joint** – biaxial, allowing movement in two planes. Example: the radiocarpal joint of the wrist.
- **Gliding joint** –two flat surfaces glide over one another, permitting movement in most directions, although mainly biaxial. Example: the carpal bones in the wrist.
- **Saddle joint** – a concave surface meets a convex surface. The joint is biaxial. Example: carpal–metacarpal joint of the thumb.
- **Ball-and-socket joint** – allows a wide range of movement and occurs when a round head of bone fits into a cup-shaped depression. Example: the shoulder joint.

4.2 Muscles

Muscles are crucial to movements in sports. There are three types of muscle:

- **Involuntary muscle**, also known as **smooth muscle**, is found in the body's internal organs. It is called involuntary muscle because it is not under our conscious control.
- **Cardiac muscle** is found only in the heart. It is also involuntary muscle.
- **Skeletal** (or **voluntary**) **muscle** is under our conscious control and is used primarily for movement.

Since skeletal muscle is the muscle type that is most important for movement in sport, let us look at its structure in more detail.

Skeletal muscle

Skeletal muscle can lengthen when contracting – it has 'extensibility'. Skeletal muscle is also very elastic and returns to its normal (resting) length after stretching. Skeletal muscle can also contract (shorten) forcibly after being stimulated by the nervous or hormonal systems.

Skeletal muscle has three important functions:
- movement
- support and posture
- heat production.

Skeletal muscle fibres

There are three types of muscle fibre. They have particular characteristics that affect performance in sport:

Type 1 – slow oxidative fibres (slow-twitch fibres)
- Red in colour.
- Contract slowly – myelin sheath of motor neurone not as thick therefore slows nerve impulse.
- Exert less force.
- Aerobic – mainly concerned with endurance.
- Can contract repeatedly.

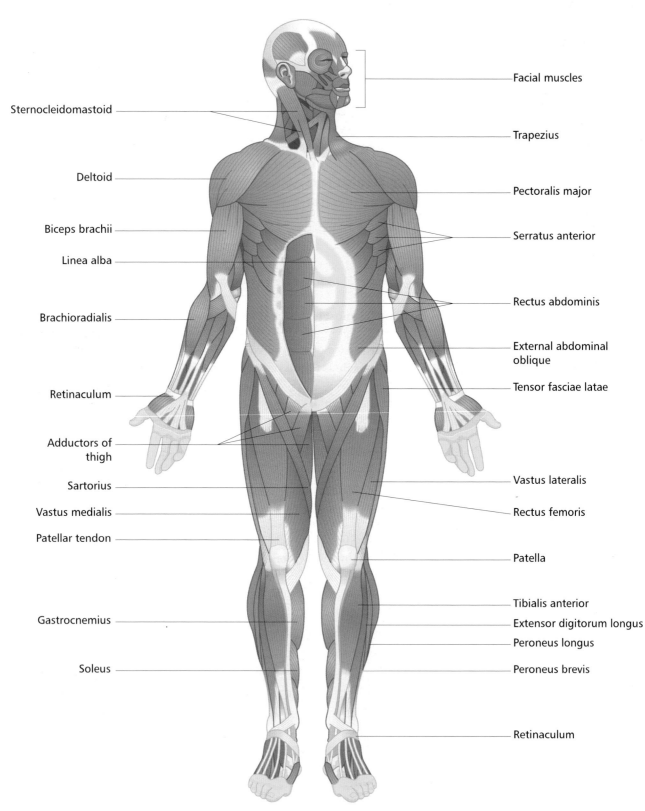

Figure 4.5 Muscles of the body – anterior view

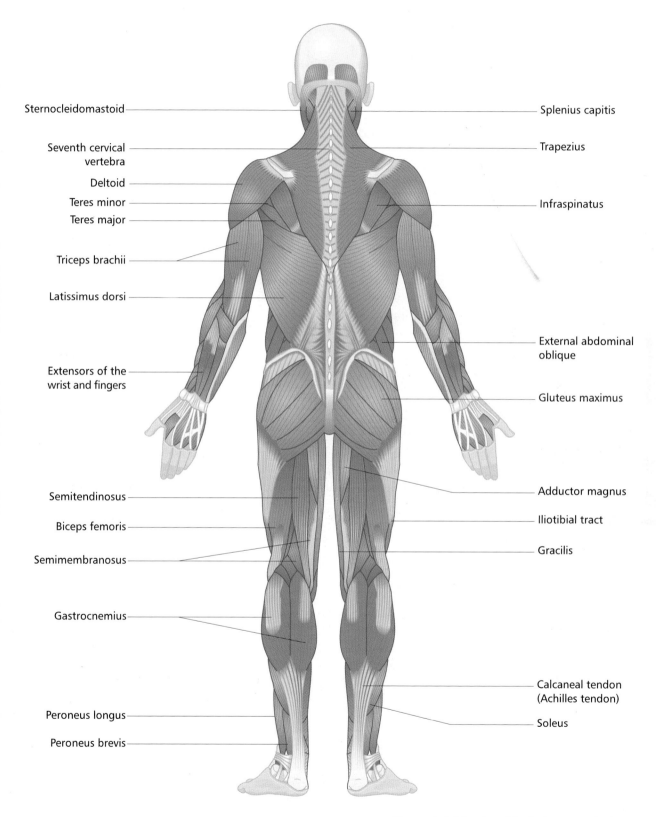

Sternocleidomastoid

Seventh cervical vertebra

Deltoid

Teres minor

Teres major

Triceps brachii

Latissimus dorsi

Extensors of the wrist and fingers

Semitendinosus

Biceps femoris

Semimembranosus

Gastrocnemius

Peroneus longus

Peroneus brevis

Splenius capitis

Trapezius

Infraspinatus

External abdominal oblique

Gluteus maximus

Adductor magnus

Iliotibial tract

Gracilis

Calcaneal tendon (Achilles tendon)

Soleus

Figure 4.6 Muscles of the body – posterior view

Type 2a – fast oxidative glycolytic fibres (fast-twitch fibres)
- White in colour.
- Contract quicker than slow-twitch – thicker myelin sheath.
- Exert more force – more muscle fibres in each motor unit.
- Aerobic and anaerobic but much more anaerobic – release energy quickly.
- Fatigue quickly.

Type 2b – fast glycolytic fibres (fast-twitch fibres)
- White in colour.
- Contract quickly.
- Exert large amount of force – motor neurone that carries impulse is much larger.
- Mostly anaerobic – less aerobic than 2a.
- Fatigue extremely quickly.

Every individual has a different mix of these fibres. This accounts for why some people are 'naturally' fast runners, whereas others seem to be 'natural' long-distance runners.

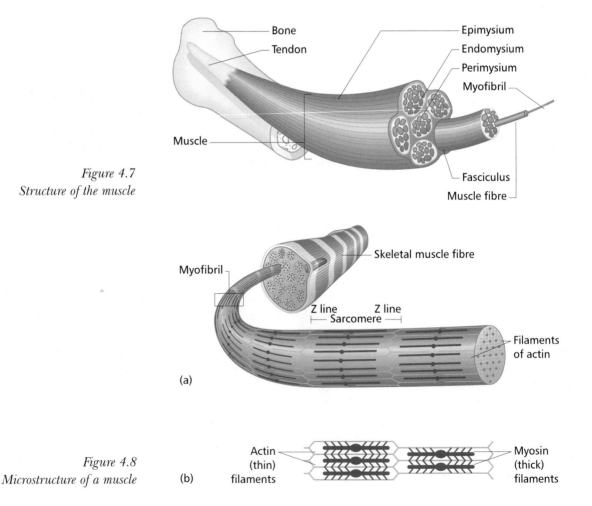

Figure 4.7
Structure of the muscle

Figure 4.8
Microstructure of a muscle

Sliding filament theory

This theory was put forward by Huxley in 1969 to explain how a muscle alters its length. When a muscle contracts:

- the I band shortens
- the A band remains the same length
- the H band disappears.

The myosin pulls the actin across so that the two filaments slide closer together, but the filaments do not actually get any shorter.

For a more detailed analysis of the sliding filament theory see Honeybourne 2000, pages 31–32.

All or none law

The strength of the stimulus is important in muscle contraction – if it is strong enough to activate at least one motor unit then *all* the fibres within that unit will contract. Neurones and muscle fibres either respond completely – **all** – or not at all – **none**.

When viewed under a microscope (see Figure 4.6), the 'belly' of the muscle is surrounded by a layer of thick connective tissue called the **epimysium**. The muscle is made up of bundles of fibres called **fasciculi**. Every fibre is composed of many smaller fibres called **myofibrils**, which are long tubular structures. Myofibrils have dark and light bands (or striations), which make up a **sarcomere**.

The sarcomeres are the contractile units of the muscle. In each sarcomere there are two protein filaments – **myosin** (thick filaments) and the thinner **actin**.

The sarcomere and the myofibril striations are shown in Figure 4.7.

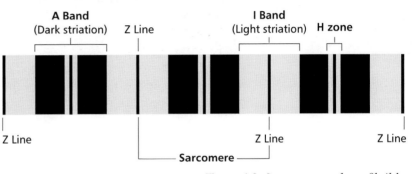

Figure 4.9 Sarcomeres and myofibril bands

The sarcomere is indicated between the two **Z lines**. The **I band** contains only thin actin filaments. The **H zone** contains only myosin filaments and the **A band** contains both actin and myosin filaments.

The interaction between actin and myosin during muscle contraction is known as the **sliding filament theory**.

Muscular contraction

Muscular contraction involves the interaction of muscles with the nervous system.

- An electrical impulse is sent from the brain to the muscles via the spinal cord and nerve cells called **motor neurones**.
- One motor neurone stimulates a number of fibres within the muscle to contract. The neurone and the fibres that have been stimulated are called a **motor unit**.
- The number of fibres that are activated (innervated) by a single motor unit depends on how finely controlled the movement has to be.
- The fibres in any given motor unit are usually either slow-twitch or fast-twitch, so the different motor units triggered depend on the type of movement that is needed.
- Once a motor unit is stimulated all the fibres within it will contract – this is called the **all or none law**.

Figure 4.10

Definition

The anatomical position

This refers to a person standing upright, facing forward, arms hanging downward, with the palms of the hands facing forward.

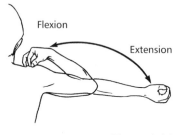

Figure 4.11

4.3 Movement analysis

The analysis of movement is very important when trying to teach skills and improve performance in sport. A good working knowledge of the terms and definitions used in movement analysis is necessary to optimise sports performance.

Movement patterns

The movements that occur around synovial joints are classified according to the actions or movement patterns they produce. Movements are described often in relation to the **anatomical position**.

- **Flexion** – a decrease in the angle around a joint. For example, from the anatomical position, bend your arm at the elbow and touch your shoulder with your hand.
- **Extension** – when the angle of the articulating bones is increased. For example, when standing up from a squat position the angle between your femur and tibia increases – extension has taken place. **Hyperextension** occurs when the angle between the articulating bones goes beyond 180°.

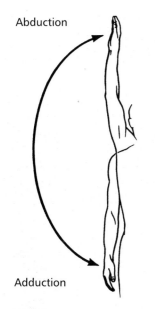

Abduction

Adduction

Figure 4.12

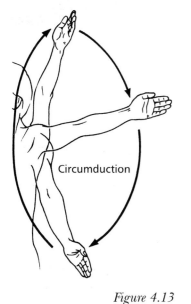

Circumduction

Figure 4.13

- **Abduction** – movement of the body away from the midline of the body. An example would be lying on your left side and lifting your right leg straight up away from the midline.
- **Adduction** – the opposite of abduction; movement towards the midline of the body. Lowering the leg that you have abducted is an example.
- **Circumduction** – when the lower end of a bone moves in the shape of a circle. This is really a combination of flexion, extension, abduction and adduction. True circumduction occurs only at the shoulder and hips, where there are ball-and-socket joints.
- **Rotation** – when the bone turns about its longitudinal axis within a joint. Rotation towards the body is called **internal** or **medial rotation**; rotation away from the body is called **external** or **lateral rotation**.
- **Pronation** – occurs at the elbow and involves internal rotation between the radius and the humerus. Facing the palm of your hand downwards is an example.
- **Supination** – the opposite of pronation; facing the palm of your hand upwards.
- **Plantarflexion** – occurs at the ankle joint when you point your toes.
- **Dorsiflexion** – also occurs at the ankle, when you bend the foot up towards your tibia.
- **Inversion** – when you turn the sole of your foot inwards towards the midline of your body the movement at the ankle is known as inversion.
- **Eversion** – the opposite of inversion; it occurs when the sole of the foot is turned outwards.
- **Elevation** – occurs at the shoulder joint when the shoulders move upwards.
- **Depression** – occurs at the shoulder joint when the shoulders move downwards.

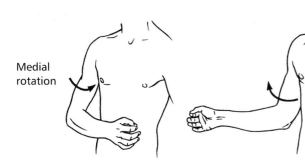

Medial rotation

Lateral rotation

Supination

Pronation

Figure 4.14

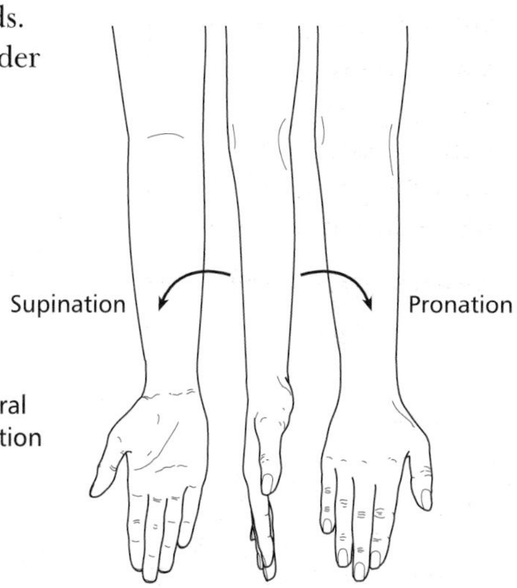

Figure 4.15

49

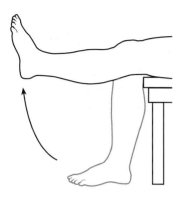

Figure 4.16 Concentric and eccentric contraction

Origin

The end of the muscle attached to a bone that is stationary, e.g. the scapula. The origin remains still when contraction occurs. Some muscles have two or more origins, e.g. the biceps has two heads, which pull on the one insertion to lift the lower arm.

Insertion

This is the end of the muscle that is attached to the bone that moves. For example, the insertion of the biceps is on the radius, which moves when the muscle contracts.

Types of muscular contraction and actions

The human body can carry out a vast range of movements. To produce these movements, muscles shorten, lengthen or remain the same length when they contract. There are four types of muscular contraction:

- **Isotonic** or **concentric contraction**. A muscle shortens and creates movement around a joint.
- **Eccentric contraction**. In eccentric contraction the muscles lengthen when contraction takes place. It acts to control movement.
- **Isometric contraction**. This occurs when a muscle contracts but there is no change in its length. During this contraction there is no movement around the joint. This is important when the muscle is acting as a **fixator**.
- **Isokinetic contraction**. In this type of contraction the muscle shortens and increases in tension whilst working at a constant speed against a variable resistance (see Honeybourne, 2000).

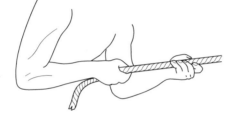

Figure 4.17

Figure 4.18

Types of muscle

Agonist

This is the muscle that produces the desired joint movement. It is also known as the **prime mover**. For example biceps brachii, which is the muscle that produces flexion at the elbow, acts as the agonist.

Antagonist

For movement to be co-ordinated and control maintained, muscles work in pairs. The movement caused by the agonist is countered by the action of the opposing muscle – the **antagonist**. For example, the action at the elbow caused by the biceps shortening is opposed by the lengthening of the triceps, which is the antagonist.

Fixator

A fixator is a muscle that works with others to stabilise the **origin** of the prime mover. For example, the trapezius contracts to stabilise the origin of the biceps.

Synergists

Synergists are the muscles that actively help the prime mover (agonist) to produce the desired movement. They are sometimes called **neutralisers** because they prevent any undesired movements. Sometimes the fixator and the synergist are the same muscle. For instance, the brachialis acts as a synergist when the elbow is bent and the forearm moves upwards.

In practice

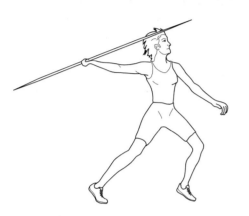

Figure 4.19

Figure 4.20

Figure 4.21

Figure 4.22

Figure 4.24

Figure 4.23

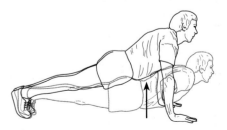

Figure 4.25

4.4 The cardiovascular system

This system provides the means of transporting oxygen, food and waste products around the body. It is very important that the athlete and coach understand how the cardiovascular system works so that performance can be maximised. The cardiovascular system includes the heart, the network of blood vessels and, of course, the blood that transports vital materials around the body.

The heart

The heart is about the size of a closed fist, comprises four chambers and consists almost entirely of cardiac muscle. The heart can be seen as incorporating two separate pumps whose main function is to pump blood around the body. The right side sends **deoxygenated blood** to the lungs and the left side sends **oxygenated blood** to the organs of the body. A muscular wall called a **septum** separates the two pumps. The muscular wall of the heart is called the **myocardium** and is found between the inner **endocardium** and the outer membrane (the **pericardium**).

The two chambers at the superior (top) part of the heart are the **atria**. The two inferior (lower) chambers are the **ventricles**.

> **Definition**
>
> **Cardiovascular**
>
> **Cardio** – means heart.
>
> **Vascular** – circulatory networks of the blood vessels.

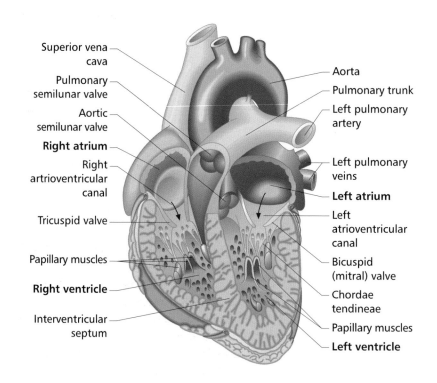

Superior vena cava
Pulmonary semilunar valve
Aortic semilunar valve
Right atrium
Right artrioventricular canal
Tricuspid valve
Papillary muscles
Right ventricle
Interventricular septum

Aorta
Pulmonary trunk
Left pulmonary artery
Left pulmonary veins
Left atrium
Left atrioventricular canal
Bicuspid (mitral) valve
Chordae tendineae
Papillary muscles
Left ventricle

Figure 4.26
Internal structure of the heart

There are many blood vessels associated with the heart. The inferior and superior **venae cavae** bring deoxygenated blood from the body to the right atrium. The **pulmonary veins** bring oxygenated blood from the lungs to the left atrium. The **pulmonary artery** takes deoxygenated blood from the right

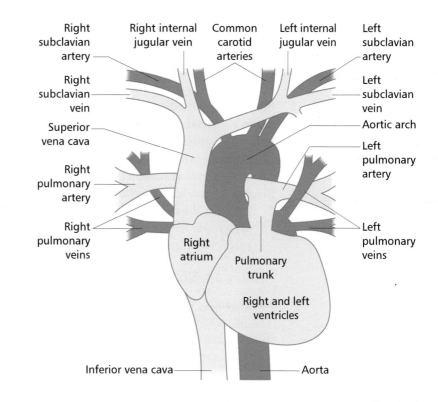

Figure 4.27 External view of the heart

ventricle to the lungs. The **aorta** takes oxygenated blood from the left ventricle to the rest of the body.

Like other muscles the heart requires a blood supply. It obtains oxygenated blood via the **coronary artery**; deoxygenated blood is taken away from the heart and into the right atrium through the **coronary sinus**.

Within the heart are a number of valves, which ensure that the blood can only flow in one direction. There are four valves within the heart – two separating the atria from the ventricles, and two in the arteries carrying blood from the ventricles. To stop the backflow of blood, the valves work only one way. The blood that flows from the atria to the ventricles pushes the valves open; the valves are then closed by connective tissue called **chordae tendineae**.

- **Atrioventricular valves** – a collective term for all the valves between the atria and ventricles.
- **Tricuspid valve** – valve between the right atrium and the right ventricle.
- **Bicuspid valve** – valve between the left atrium and the left ventricle.
- **Aortic valve** – valve between the left ventricle and the aorta.
- **Pulmonary valve** – valve between the right ventricle and the pulmonary artery
- **Semilunar valves** – collective term for aortic and pulmonary valves.

The cardiac cycle

The term 'cardiac cycle' refers to the process of the heart contracting and the transportation of blood through the heart. The cardiac cycle is a sequence of events during one complete heartbeat, including the filling of the heart with blood and the emptying of the heart.

Each cycle takes approximately 0.8 seconds. There are about 72 cycles per minute.

Stages of the cardiac cycle
Stage 1 – atrial diastole. The atria fill with blood.
Stage 2 – ventricular diastole. Blood is pumped from the atria into the ventricles through the atrioventricular valves.
Stage 3 – atrial systole. The atrioventricular valves close.
Stage 4 – ventricular systole. The semilunar valves open and the ventricles contract. Blood is forced from the right ventricle into the pulmonary artery and from the left ventricle into the aorta. Finally the semilunar valves close and the cycle is completed.

Other definitions associated with the heart and its function

Heart rate
The heart contracts and relaxes in a rhythm, which produces a heartbeat. This is started by an electrical impulse from the **sinuatrial** (SA) **node**, which is the 'pacemaker' of the heart.

Heart rate (HR) is measured by beats per minute (bpm). The average resting HR is 75 bpm.

Decrease in resting heart rate is a good indicator of fitness. A trained athlete's resting heart rate will be below 60 bpm.

Stroke volume (SV)
This is the volume of blood that is pumped out of the heart by each ventricle during one contraction. Stroke volume varies with:
- the amount of blood returning to heart (venous return)
- the elasticity of the ventricles
- the contractility of the ventricles
- the blood pressure in the arteries leading from the heart.
  SV is measured in millilitres (ml) per beat.

Cardiac output (Q)
The cardiac output is the volume of blood ejected from the left ventricle in one minute (in litres). It is a product of the stroke volume and the heart rate:

$$Q = SV \times HR$$

▌In practice
If an athlete's resting heart rate falls below 60 bpm, to produce the same cardiac output, the stroke volume has to increase to compensate for drop in heart rate. The higher the cardiac output, the more oxygen can be delivered to the muscles and the longer and harder the athlete can work.

Figure 4.28

Blood pressure (BP)

This is the pressure needed to pump the blood around the body. It is calculated by blood flow × resistance to that flow, and is measured in millimetres of mercury (mmHg).

- **Systolic BP** is measured when the heart forcibly ejects blood.
- **Diastolic BP** is measured when the heart relaxes.

The average BP in an adult is 120/80 mmHg. The first number is the systolic BP and the second number is the diastolic BP. With regular exercise resting BP can be reduced.

An instrument called a sphygmomanometer is used to take blood pressure.

Factors affecting BP include age, stress and diet.

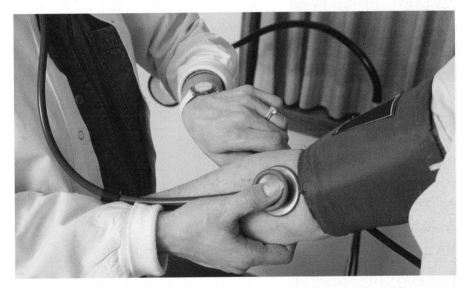

Figure 4.29
A sphygmomanometer is
used to take blood pressure

Definition

Haemoglobin

This is an iron-rich protein, which transports the oxygen in the blood. The more haemoglobin there is in an erythrocyte, the more oxygen it can carry. This concentration can be increased through endurance training.

Blood and blood vessels

The blood vessels transport blood and nutrients around the body. During exercise, most of the blood goes to the working muscles so that oxygen can be delivered and carbon dioxide taken away efficiently and effectively. Blood consists of white and red cells suspended in a liquid called **plasma**. The red cells, the **erythrocytes**, contain **haemoglobin**. Other cells in the blood are **leucocytes**, white blood cells that combat infection, and **thrombocytes** (**platelets**), which are important in the process of blood clotting.

The average total blood volume in a man is 5–6 litres and in a woman 4–5 litres.

The vascular system includes blood vessels called arteries, arterioles, capillaries, veins and venules.

Arteries and arterioles

These carry blood at high pressure from the heart to the body tissues. The largest artery is the aorta, which leaves the heart and subdivides into smaller arteries. The smaller of these vessels are called arterioles; they have a very small diameter. The walls of arteries contain muscle tissue, which can contract to increase or decrease the diameter of the arteries.

Veins and venules

These carry blood at low pressure back to the heart. Their walls are less muscular than those of the arteries, but gradually increase in thickness as they approach the heart. The vena cava is the largest vein, which enters the heart through the right atrium. The smallest veins are called venules, which transport the blood from the capillaries into the veins. Veins contain pocket valves that prevent the backflow of blood.

Capillaries

Capillaries have very thin walls – only one cell thick. This makes them thin enough for gases and nutrients to pass through them. Capillaries occur in large quantities around the muscles and this enables effective exchange of gases.

Figure 4.30
An endurance athlete

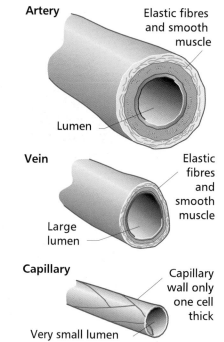

Figure 4.31 Diagram of blood vessels

Definition

Vasodilation

This occurs when the artery walls relax and the diameter of the artery increases.

Vasoconstriction

This occurs when the artery walls contract and the diameter of the artery decreases.

The vessels can therefore help to change the pressure of the blood, which is especially important during exercise.

4.5 The respiratory system

It is important to study the respiratory system in combination with the cardiovascular system because the two systems work closely together to maintain a supply of oxygen to the working muscles, which is so crucial in sport.

The **external respiratory system** involves the exchange of gases in the lungs. The **internal respiratory system** involves the exchange of gases between the blood and the cells. The term **cellular respiration** refers to the process that involves the production of adenosine triphosphate (ATP).

The organs of the respiratory system

Nasal passages

The air is drawn into the body through the nose. The nasal cavity is divided by a cartilaginous septum that forms the nasal passages. Here the mucous membranes warm and moisten the air and the hair filters and traps dust.

The pharynx and the larynx

The throat is the entry to both the respiratory and alimentary tracts, and both food and air pass through. Air passes over the vocal cords of the **larynx** and into the **trachea**. Swallowing draws the larynx upwards against the epiglottis and prevents food going into the trachea. Any food is sent down the oesophagus.

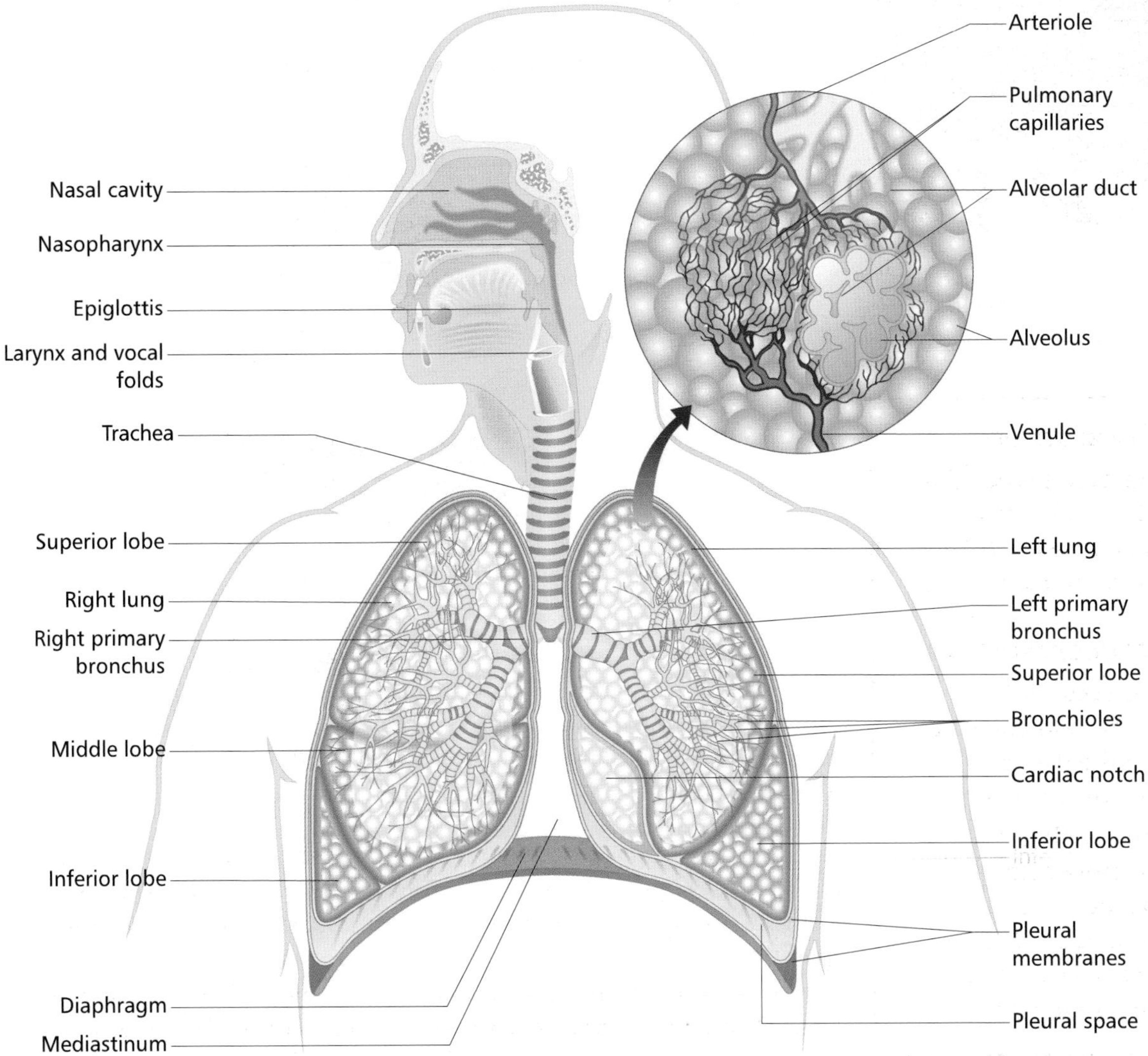
Arteriole
Pulmonary capillaries
Alveolar duct
Alveolus
Venule
Nasal cavity
Nasopharynx
Epiglottis
Larynx and vocal folds
Trachea
Superior lobe
Right lung
Right primary bronchus
Middle lobe
Inferior lobe
Diaphragm
Mediastinum
Left lung
Left primary bronchus
Superior lobe
Bronchioles
Cardiac notch
Inferior lobe
Pleural membranes
Pleural space

Figure 4.32 The respiratory system

The trachea

This is sometimes called the windpipe. It is lined with a mucous membrane and ciliated cells, which trap dust, and contains 18 rings of cartilage to keep it open and protect it. The trachea goes from the larynx to the primary bronchi.

The bronchi and bronchioles

The trachea divides into two **bronchi** – the right bronchus goes into the right lung and the left bronchus goes into the left lung. The bronchi then divide up into smaller **bronchioles**. The bronchioles enable the air to pass into the **alveoli**, where diffusion takes place.

Alveoli

These tiny air-filled sacs are the site of gaseous exchange between the lungs and the blood. There are many million alveoli in the lungs, which provides an enormous surface area (some have estimated the size of a tennis court!). The walls of the alveoli are extremely thin and moist, which allows oxygen from the inspired air to dissolve. The exchange of oxygen is illustrated in Figure 4.33.

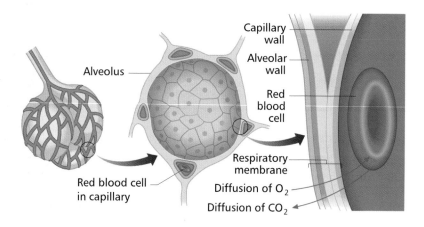

Figure 4.33 Gaseous exchange between an alveolus and capillary bed

The lungs

These lie in the thoracic cavity, which is protected by the ribs and separated into two by the mediastinum (which contains the heart). The **pleural membrane** that lines the pleural cavity surrounds each of the two lungs. The pleural cavity contains **pleural fluid**, which reduces friction on the lungs when breathing. The **diaphragm** borders the bottom of the lungs and is a sheet of skeletal muscle.

Breathing

Inspiration

- The respiratory muscles contract. These include the external intercostal muscles and the diaphragm. The external intercostal muscles are attached to the ribs, and when they contract the ribs move upwards and outwards.

- The diaphragm contracts and moves downward, increasing the volume of the thoracic cavity.
- The lungs are pulled outwards along with the chest walls through surface tension, which causes the space within the lungs to increase.
- The pressure within the lungs decreases and becomes less than the pressure outside the body.
- Gases move from areas of high pressure into areas of low pressure and so air passes into the lungs.

In practice

*During exercise the **sternocleidomastoid** lifts the sternum; the **scalenes** and **pectoralis minor** both elevate the ribs. These actions help to increase the size of the thoracic cavity.*

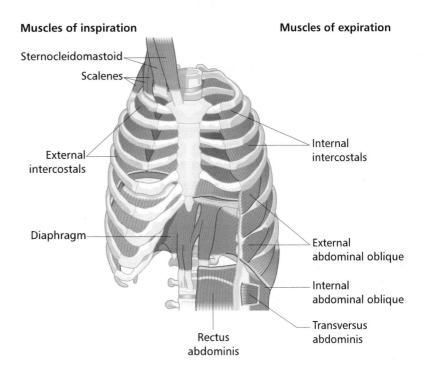

Muscles of inspiration   Muscles of expiration

Sternocleidomastoid

Scalenes

External intercostals

Internal intercostals

Diaphragm

External abdominal oblique

Internal abdominal oblique

Transversus abdominis

Rectus abdominis

Figure 4.34 Muscles involved in respiration

Expiration

This is more of a passive process than inspiration.

- The respiratory muscles relax. When the external intercostal muscles relax, the ribs are lowered and the diaphragm relaxes.
- The volume of the lungs decreases and the pressure within the lungs becomes greater than the pressure outside the body.
- Air is now forced out to equalise this pressure.

Gaseous exchange

At the lungs

Gases diffuse across the respiratory membrane because of the imbalance in concentration between the various gases in the alveoli and the blood.

Oxygen diffuses from the alveoli into the blood and carbon dioxide diffuses from the blood into the alveoli. Athletes who are involved with endurance events have a greater ability to diffuse oxygen because they have a higher cardiac output and a larger surface area of alveoli.

At the muscles

The concentration of oxygen in the blood is higher than in the tissues, so it diffuses through the capillary wall and into the muscle cytoplasm. Carbon dioxide moves in the opposite direction. When oxygen is in the muscle it attaches itself to **myoglobin**, which takes the oxygen to the mitochondria and cellular respiration takes place to produce energy.

Lung volumes

The volume of air that is inspired and expired is known as the **tidal volume** (TV). The volume of air that is inspired and expired in one minute is called the **minute ventilation** ($\dot{V}_E$). This is calculated by multiplying tidal volume by the number of breaths per minute:

$$\dot{V}_E = \text{TV} \times \text{frequency}$$

It is measured in litres/minute.

The lungs can never completely get rid of all the air – approximately 1200 ml remains in the alveoli. This is called the **reserve volume**.

4.6 Short-term responses and long-term adaptations to exercise

Short-term responses

The cardiovascular system

The following short-term responses occur in the cardiovascular system:

- **Heart rate changes**. There is an anticipatory rise due to hormonal action, and then there is a sharp rise due to sensory stimulation and hormones. The heart rate continues high due to maximal workloads – this is a period of steady state. As exercise decreases there is a fall in heart rate due to withdrawal of stimuli and drop in hormone levels. Eventually the heart rate returns to the resting rate.
- **Breathing rate rises** due to demands for more oxygen.

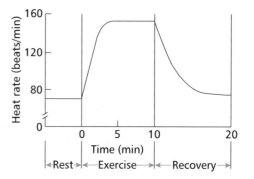

Figure 4.35 Changes in heart rate with submaximal exercise

The respiratory system

During exercise:

- Tidal volume (TV) increases.
- Inspiratory reserve volume (the maximal volume inspired in addition to the tidal volume) decreases.
- Expiratory reserve volume (the maximal volume expired in addition to the tidal volume) decreases slightly.
- Residual volume (the amount of air left in the lungs after maximal expiration) slightly increases.
- Total lung capacity, the volume at the end of maximal inspiration (the vital capacity plus the residual volume), slightly decreases.
- Vital capacity (the maximum amount of air that can be forcibly exhaled after maximal inspiration) slightly decreases.

Long-term adaptations

The following long-term adaptations may occur due to exercise.

- Increase in bone density.
- Increase in numbers of capillaries and increase in efficiency of gaseous exchange.
- Lowering of resting heart rate.
- Increase in vital capacity.
- Aerobic adaptations in muscle: activities such as swimming or running can enlarge the slow-twitch fibres, which gives greater potential for energy production.
    - size and number of mitochondria increase
    - increase in myoglobin content within the muscle cell
    - onset of fatigue is delayed because of higher maximum oxygen uptake (VO_2 max.)
- Anaerobic adaptations in muscle:
    - activities like sprinting or weightlifting can cause **hypertrophy** of fast-twitch muscle fibres
    - size of heart increases – called **cardiac hypertrophy**.
- Increase in stroke volume at rest and during exercise.
- Increase in cardiac output.
- Decrease in resting blood pressure
- Increase in haemoglobin, which helps carry oxygen along with increase in red blood cells.

    For exercise and training factors that affect adaptations, see Chapter 7.

Progress check

1   Name four main functions of the skeleton.
2   Describe four different types of cancellous bone.
3   What is cartilage and why is it so important to the sports participant?
4   Draw a fully labelled diagram of a synovial joint.

5 Explain, using examples from sport, the importance of skeletal muscle.

6 Describe Type A, Type 2a and Type 2b skeletal muscle fibres.

7 Using an example of a simple movement in sport, describe the process of muscle contraction.

8 Give definitions of flexion, extension, adduction and abduction.

9 Describe the type of muscle contraction in a simple skill related to sport.

10 Draw a diagram of the heart.

11 What is meant by the cardiac cycle?

12 What does stroke volume depend upon?

13 Describe haemoglobin. Why is it so important in sport?

14 Draw a diagram of the lungs.

15 Describe gaseous exchange at the muscles.

16 Give three short-term responses and three long-term adaptations to exercise.

5 Nutrition and weight management in sport

This chapter covers the necessary information required by the BTEC specifications for the units related to nutrition and sport and nutrition and weight management. The information in this chapter will enable students to give advice to sportspeople wanting to lose body fat and gain muscle mass. Suitable nutritional strategies will be explored. The importance of a healthy diet will be investigated and the links between diet and health discussed. The dietary requirements of athletes involved in a variety of sports during training and competition are studied. Nutritional supplements and their use in helping sports performance will be investigated. After considering the information in this chapter students will be able to evaluate the effectiveness of sportspeople's diets.

The importance of nutrition in weight management is also covered and issues such as obesity, coronary heart disease and anorexia nervosa are studied.

Learning objectives

- To investigate the components and importance of a healthy diet.
- To investigate nutritional strategies for sportspeople.
- To explore factors that affect weight management.

5.1 Components of a healthy diet

The main components essential for a healthy diet are:
- carbohydrates
- fats
- proteins
- vitamins
- minerals
- water.

Carbohydrates

These are made up of the chemical elements of carbon, hydrogen and oxygen only. Carbohydrates are primarily involved in energy production. There are two forms of carbohydrate:

- Simple sugars – these provide a quick energy source and include glucose and fructose.
- Complex starches – these have many sugar units and are much slower in releasing energy.

Carbohydrates are very important to the athlete, especially in exercise that is highly intense. Carbohydrates are also essential to the nervous system and fat metabolism.

Carbohydrates are stored in the muscles and the liver as glycogen but in limited amounts that need to be replenished.

▌▌▌ *In practice*

If exercise levels are below 95% of the athlete's V_{O_2} max (see Chapter 4), both carbohydrates and fats are used as fuels. Above this intensity, carbohydrates appear to be used exclusively; thus a fast pace in early stages of exercise may lead to glycogen depletion and premature exhaustion.

Sources of carbohydrates:

- **Complex** – cereal, pasta, potatoes, bread, fruit.
- **Simple** – sugar, jam, confectionery, fruit juices.

During exercise glycogen is broken down to the glucose that supplies muscles with energy. When glycogen stores are depleted, there is less energy available and the athlete will become fatigued. It is recommended that carbohydrates should make up about 60% of a sportsperson's diet.

Fats

These are a major source of energy, especially for athletes performing low-intensity endurance exercise. Fats and lipids are made up of carbon, hydrogen and oxygen but in different proportions to carbohydrates. There are two types:

- Triglycerides – stored in the form of body fat.
- Fatty acids – used mainly as fuel for energy production. These are either **saturated** or **unsaturated**.

When muscle cells are readily supplied with oxygen, fat is the usual fuel for energy production. This is because the body is trying to save the limited stores of glycogen for high-intensity exercise and delay the onset of fatigue. However, the body cannot solely use fat for energy and so the muscle is fuelled by a combination of fat and glycogen.

▌▌▌ *In practice*

When a marathon runner 'hits the wall' his or her glycogen stores are depleted and the body attempts to metabolise fat, which is a slower way of producing energy. Therefore the athlete experiences extreme fatigue and the muscles struggle to contract.

Definition

Saturated and unsaturated fats

Saturated fats are usually solid (e.g. lard) and primarily from animal sources. Unsaturated fats are usually liquid (e.g. vegetable oil) and come from plant sources.

Figure 5.1 Fat consumption should be carefully monitored

Fat consumption should be carefully monitored – too much can cause obesity (which will be dealt with later in this chapter). Fat is very important – it protects vital organs and is crucial for cell production and the control of heat loss. Generally, a maximum of 30% of total calories consumed should be from fatty foods.

Sources of fats:

- Saturated fats – meat products, dairy products, cakes, confectionery.
- Unsaturated fats – oily fish, nuts, margarine, olive oil.

Protein

Proteins are chemical compounds that consist of **amino acids**, composed of carbon, hydrogen, oxygen and nitrogen and some contain minerals such as zinc. Proteins are known as the building blocks for body tissue and are essential for repair. They are also necessary for the production of enzymes and hormones. Proteins can be used as a source of energy but only if fats and carbohydrates are in very short supply.

Protein should account for approximately 15% of total calorific intake. If excessive protein is taken then there are some health risks – for example kidney damage due to excreting so many unused amino acids.

Sources of protein:

- Meat, fish and poultry are the three primary sources of **complete** proteins.
- The proteins obtained from vegetables and grains are called **incomplete** proteins because they do not supply all the essential amino acids.

In practice

Protein breaks down more readily during and immediately after exercise. The amount of protein broken down depends upon the duration and intensity of exercise. Increased protein intake may be necessary during the early stages of training to support increases in muscle mass and myoglobin.

Vitamins

Vitamins are non-caloric chemical compounds that are needed by the body in only small quantities. They are an essential component of our diet because they are used in the production of energy, prevention of disease and metabolism. With the exception of vitamin D the body cannot produce vitamins. Vitamins A,D,E and K are fat-soluble vitamins. Vitamins B and C are water-soluble vitamins.

Vitamins can be found in fresh fruit and vegetables.

In practice

To ensure you don't destroy the vitamins in your food:

- *Buy good-quality fresh fruit and vegetables.*
- *Wash/scrub food rather than peeling it because vitamins are often found just below the skin.*
- *Prepare just before cooking and boil in as little water as possible. Steaming or microwave cooking is better.*
- *Eat soon after cooking.*

Definition

Amino acids

These are the building blocks of proteins. There are ten amino acids that we are unable to make for ourselves: these are called essential amino acids. Examples are leucine and threonine. We have to take in the essential amino acids as part of our diet. The other twelve amino acids are called non-essential, because we can manufacture them. Examples are glycine and glutamine.

Table 5.1 The major vitamins and their functions

Vitamin	RDA for healthy adult (milligrams)	Dietary sources	Major body functions	Deficiency disease	Symptoms of excess
Water-soluble vitamins					
B1 (thiamine)	1.4–1.5 (M), 1.0–1.1 (F)	Pork, organ meats, whole grains, legumes	Coenzyme in reactions involving the removal of carbon dioxide	Beri beri (peripheral nerve changes, oedema, heart failure)	None reported
B2 (riboflavin)	1.6–1.7 (M), 1.2–1.3 (F)	Widely distributed in foods	Constituent of two coenzymes involved in energy metabolism	Reddened lips, cracks at corner of mouth, lesions of eye	None reported
Niacin	18–19 (M), 13–14 (F)	Liver, lean meats, grains, legumes (can be formed from tryptophan)	Constituent of two coenzymes involved in oxidation-reduction reactions	Pellagra (skin and gastrointestinal lesions, nervous and mental disorders)	Flushing, burning and tingling around neck, face and hands
B6 (pyridoxine)	2.2 (M), 2.0 (F)	Meats, vegetables, whole-grain cereals	Coenzyme involved in amino acid metabolism	Irritability, convulsions, muscular twitching, dermatitis near eyes, kidney stones	None reported
Pantothenic acid	4–7 (M, F)	Widely distributed in foods	Constituent of coenzyme A, which plays a central role in energy metabolism	Fatigue, sleep disturbances, impaired coordination, nausea (rare in humans)	None reported
Folic acid	0.4 (M, F)	Legumes, green vegetables, whole-wheat products	Coenzyme involved in transfer of single-carbon units in nucleic acid and amino acid metabolism	Anaemia, gastrointestinal disturbances, diarrhoea, red tongue	None reported
B12	0.003 (M, F)	Muscle meats, eggs, dairy products (not present in plant foods)	Coenzyme involved in transfer of single-carbon units in nucleic acid metabolism	Pernicious anaemia, neurological disorders	None reported
Biotin	0.1–0.2 (M, F)	Legumes, vegetables, meats	Coenzyme required for fat synthesis, amino acid metabolism and glycogen formation	Fatigue, depression, nausea, dermatitis, muscle pains	None reported
C (ascorbic acid)	60 (M, F)	Citrus fruits, tomatoes, green peppers, salad greens	Maintains intercellular matrix of cartilage, bone and dentine. Important in collagen synthesis	Scurvy (degeneration of skin, teeth, blood vessels, epithelial haemorrhages)	Relatively non-toxic. Possibility of kidney stones

Table 5.1 continued

Fat-soluble vitamins

Vitamin	RDA for healthy adult (milligrams)	Dietary sources	Major body functions	Deficiency disease	Symptoms of excess
A (retinol)	1.0 (M), 0.8 (F)	Provitamin A (beta carotene) widely distributed in green vegetables. Retinol present in milk, butter, cheese, fortified margarine	Constituent of rhodopsin (visual pigment). Maintenance of epithelial role in mucopolysaccharide synthesis	Xerophthalmia (keratinisation of ocular tissue), night blindness, permanent blindness	Headache, vomiting, peeling of skin, anorexia, swelling of long bones
D	0.075 (M, F)	Cod-liver oil, eggs, dairy products, fortified milk and margarine	Promotes growth and mineralisation of bones. Increases absorption of calcium	Rickets (bone deformities) in children. Osteomalacia in adults	Vomiting, diarrhoea, loss of weight, kidney damage
E (tocopherol)	10 (M), 8 (F)	Seeds, green leafy vegetables, margarines, shortenings	Functions as an antioxidant to prevent cell membrane damage	Possibly anaemia	Relatively non-toxic
K (phylloquinone)	0.07–0.14 (M, F)	Green leafy vegetables. Small amount in cereals, fruit and meats	Important in blood clotting (involved in formation of active prothrombin)	Conditioned deficiencies associated with severe bleeding; internal haemorrhages	Relatively non-toxic. Synthetic forms at high doses may cause jaundice

RDA = recommended daily amount; M = male; f = female

Table 5.2 The major minerals

Mineral	Amount in adult body (g)	RDA for healthy adult (milligrams)	Dietary sources	Major body functions	Deficiency disease	Symptoms of excess
Calcium	1500	800 (M, F)	Milk, cheese, dark green vegetables, dried legumes	Bone and tooth formation, blood clotting, nerve transmission	Stunted growth, rickets, osteoporosis, convulsions	Not reported in humans
Phosphorus	860	800 (M, F)	Milk, cheese, meat, poultry, grains	Bone and tooth formation, acid–base balance	Weakness, demineralisation of bone, loss of calcium	Erosion of bone (fossy jaw)
Sulphur	300	Provided by sulphur amino acids	Sulphur amino acids (methionine and cystine) in dietary proteins	Constituent of active tissue compounds, cartilage and tendon	Related to intake and deficiency of sulphur amino acids	Excess sulphur amino acid intake leads to poor growth
Potassium	180	1875–5625	Meats, milk, many fruits	Acid–base balance, body water balance, nerve function	Muscular weakness, paralysis	Muscular weakness, death
Chlorine	74	1700–5100	Common salt	Formation of gastric juice, acid–base balance	Muscle cramps, mental apathy, reduced appetite	Vomiting
Sodium	64	1100–3300	Common salt	Acid–base balance, body water balance, nerve function	Muscle cramps, mental apathy, reduced appetite	High blood pressure
Magnesium	25	350 (M), 300 (F)	Whole grains, green leafy vegetables	Activates enzymes involved in protein synthesis	Growth failure, behavioural disturbances, weakness, spasms	Diarrhoea
Iron	4.5	10 (M), 18 (F)	Eggs, lean meat, legumes, whole grains, green leafy vegetables	Constituent of haemoglobin and enzymes involved in energy metabolism	Iron-deficiency anaemia (weakness, reduces resistance to infection)	Siderosis, cirrhosis of liver
Fluorine	2.6	1.5–4.0	Drinking water, tea, seafood	May be important in maintenance of bone structure	Higher frequency of tooth decay	Mottling of teeth, increased bone density, neurological disturbances
Zinc	2	15	Widely distributed in foods	Constituent of enzymes involved in digestion	Growth failure, small sex glands	Fever, nausea, vomiting, diarrhoea

Table 5.2 continued

Mineral	Amount in adult body (g)	RDA for healthy adult (milligrams)	Dietary sources	Major body functions	Deficiency disease	Symptoms of excess
Copper	0.1	2	Meats, drinking water	Constituent of enzymes associated with iron	Anaemia, bone changes (rare in humans)	Rare metabolic condition (Wilson's disease)
Silicon, vanadium, tin, nickel	0.024, 0.018, 0.17, 0.010	Not established	Widely distributed in foods	Function unknown (essential for animals)	Not reported in humans	Industrial exposures: silicon – silicosis, vanadium – lung irritation, tin – vomiting, nickel – acute pneumonitis
Selenium	0.013	0.02–0.05	Seafood, meat, grains	Functions in close association with vitamin E	Anaemia (rare)	Gastrointestinal disorders, lung irritation
Manganese	0.012	Not established (diet provides 6–8g per day)	Widely distributed in foods	Constituent of enzymes involved in fat synthesis	In animals: poor growth, disturbances of nervous system, reproductive abnormalities	Poisoning in manganese mines: generalised disease of nervous system
Iodine	0.011	0.15	Marine fish and shellfish, dairy products, many vegetables	Constituent of thyroid hormones	Goitre (enlarged thyroid)	Very high intakes depress thyroid activity
Molybdenum	0.009	Not established (diet provides 0.4 per day)	Legumes, cereals, organ meats	Constituent of some enzymes	Impaired ability to metabolise glucose	Occupational exposures: skin and kidney damage
Cobalt	0.0015	(Required as vitamin B12)	Organ and muscle meats, milk	Constituent of vitamin B12	Not reported in humans	Industrial exposure: dermatitis and diseases of red blood cells
Water	40 000 (60% of body weight)	1.5 litres per day	Solid foods, liquids, drinking water	Transport of nutrients, temperature regulation, participates in metabolic reactions	Thirst, dehydration	Headaches, nausea, oedema, high blood pressure

RDA = recommended daily amount; M = male; F = female; g = grams

> **Definition**
>
> ***Antioxidant vitamins***
>
> These are beta carotene, vitamin C and vitamin E (sometimes known as the ACE vitamins). They can help prevent damage to muscles and reduce post-exercise muscle soreness.

Extremely large doses of vitamins can be dangerous – for example too much vitamin A can cause hair loss and enlargement of the liver. There is little evidence to suggest that supplementary vitamin pills can enhance performance and most excess vitamins are simply excreted in the urine. There is some evidence that hard exercise can deplete the body's stores of antioxidant vitamins.

Minerals

These are also non-caloric and are inorganic elements essential for our health. There are two types:

- **Macro-minerals** are needed in large amounts – e.g. calcium, potassium, sodium.
- **Trace elements** are needed in very small amounts – e.g. iron, zinc, manganese.

Many minerals are dissolved in the body fluids as ions (these are called **electrolytes**). Electrolytes are essential for healthy cells, the nervous system and for muscle contraction. Minerals can be lost through sweating and so people who exercise should replace them quickly to ensure good health.

Iron

This is an essential component of haemoglobin, which carries oxygen in the blood. Iron-deficiency anaemia can impair performance in endurance events. Research has shown that over 36% of female runners are anaemic and therefore should eat iron-rich foods. Only a qualified medical doctor should prescribe iron supplements because too much iron can be dangerous.

Iron can be found in meat, fish, dairy produce and green vegetables. Main sources are red meat and offal.

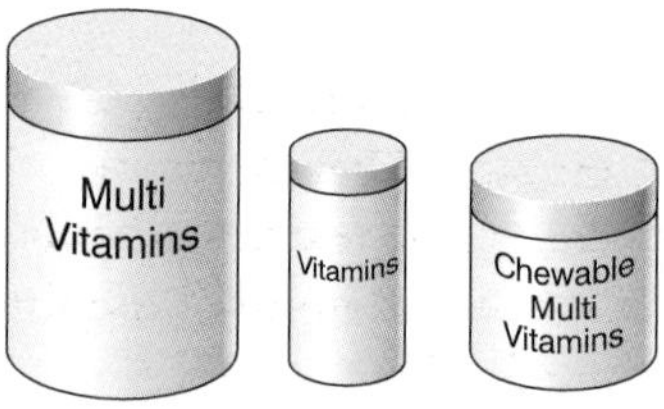

Figure 5.2

Calcium

This mineral is essential for healthy bones and teeth. If there is deficiency in calcium, then there is an increased likelihood of bone fractures and osteoporosis. For calcium to be absorbed, there needs to be sufficient vitamin D, which is produced in the body in response to sunlight.

Calcium is found in milk and dairy products, green vegetables and nuts.

> ***In practice***
>
> ***Calcium deficiency***
>
> *Calcium deficiency can be found in females who are underweight, smokers, alcoholics, vegetarians or people who overdo training in sport.*

Water

Water is also crucial for good health, particularly for those who participate in sport. It carries nutrients in the body and helps with the removal of waste products. It is also very important in the regulation of body temperature. The body readily loses water through urine and sweat. The amount of water lost depends on the environment and the duration and intensity of exercise. On average an individual should drink about two litres of water a day. People involved in exercise should take more to ensure a good state of hydration.

In practice

Individuals who are dehydrated become intolerant to exercise and heat stress. The cardiovascular system becomes inefficient if a person is dehydrated and becomes unable to provide adequate blood flow to the skin – which may lead to heat exhaustion.

Fluids must be taken in during prolonged exercise to minimise dehydration and slow the rise in body temperature.

A number of sports drinks containing electrolytes and carbohydrates are available commercially but some of the claims that are made about these drinks have been misinterpreted. A single meal, for instance, can replace the minerals lost during exercise. Water is the primary need in any drink taken before, during and after exercise because it empties from the stomach extremely quickly and reduces the dehydration associated with sweating. Thirst is not a reliable indicator for fluid intake; if you are thirsty you are already dehydrated. It is best to drink small amounts regularly even if you are not thirsty. Under cooler conditions, a carbohydrate drink may give the extra energy needed in events lasting over an hour.

5.2 Healthy eating

Food labelling

The amounts and proportions of nutrients vary enormously in different types of food. It is important for consumers to know what nutrients are present in foods so that they can make more informed choices based on health requirements.

Since 1986, all UK foods that are processed and all non-alcoholic beverages must carry a label showing a list of ingredients. This list shows the ingredients in descending order of weight, thus the first few ingredients make up most of the food. The additives are usually at the bottom of the list because they only make up a small proportion of the food.

Many manufacturers also now publish the nutritional value of the food on the labels.

Figure 5.3 Food labels reveal what is really in the packet!

In practice

The truth behind the labels

- *'Low fat' – less than 5 g in 100 g. (Note that labelling is based on percentage weight of fat in the product – not percentage of calories from fat!)*
- *'Reduced fat' – 25% or more less fat than the 'normal'.*
- *'Virtually fat free' – less than 0.3 g fat in 100 g.*
- *'Reduced sugar' – at least 25% less sugar than 'normal'.*
- *'Low sugar' – less than 5 g sugar in 100 g.*
- *'Sugar free' – no natural or added sugar.*
- *'Reduced calories' – at least 25% fewer calories than 'normal'.*
- *'Low calorie' – less than 40 calories in 100 g.*
- *'High fibre' – at least 6 g in 100 g.*

Healthy eating involves a daily calorie intake in the following proportions:

- 50% carbohydrate
- 30–35% fat
- 15–20% protein

According to the Health Development Agency (2000) the principles that should govern your food choice include:

- enjoyment
- not too much fat
- not too many sugary foods
- inclusion of vitamins and minerals
- plenty of fibre
- alcohol within prescribed limits
- maintenance of balance of intake and output
- plenty of fruit and vegetables.

In practice

Alcohol consumption

Alcohol is a concentrated source of energy but the energy cannot be available during exercise for our working muscles.

The Health Education Authority (now called the Health Development Agency) recommend the following maximum daily alcohol intakes for adults:

- *Men 3–4 units.*
- *Women 2–3 units.*

One unit:

- 1/2 pint 'ordinary strength' beer = 3.0–3.5% alcohol = 90 calories
- 1 standard glass of wine = 11% alcohol = 90 calories
- single measure spirits = 38% alcohol = 50 calories.

'Binge drinking', which is a growing habit amongst teenagers and young adults, is particularly bad for you. It is better to spread your alcohol consumption across the week and to leave some alcohol-free days.

Figure 5.4 Alcohol consumption is increasing among under 18's

A healthy diet

There are no healthy or unhealthy foods; there are only good or bad uses of food. The right balance in a diet is essential for health and fitness. Enjoyment is an important aspect of eating; a healthy diet does not mean that you have to give up all your favourite foods that are considered 'bad' foods – it is the overall balance that counts. Balanced meals contain starchy foods, plenty of vegetables, salad and fruit. Your fat content should be kept to a minimum by using low-fat or lean ingredients.

Factors that also affect choice of foods include:

- Culture; morals; ethics.
- Family influences.
- Peer group influences.

- Lifestyle.
- Finance.

⫶ *In practice*

The balance of good health model

This is a model designed by the Health Development Agency to show what healthy eating means:

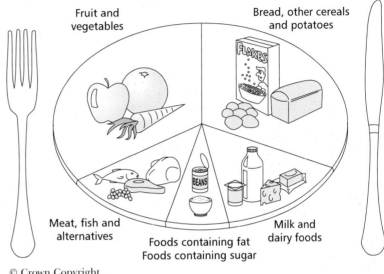

Figure 5.5 A balanced diet

© Crown Copyright

Eating sufficient fruit and vegetables is important for a healthy diet. It helps to reduce the likelihood of coronary heart disease and some cancers. Government guidelines suggest that you should eat at least five portions of fruit and vegetables each day.

⫶ *In practice*

What is a 'portion' of fruit or vegetables?
- *Two tablespoons of vegetables.*
- *One dessert bowlful of salad.*
- *One apple/orange/banana.*
- *Two plums.*
- *One cupful of grapes/cherries.*
- *Two tablespoons of fresh fruit salad.*
- *One tablespoon dried fruit.*
- *One glass fruit juice.*

Most healthy eating guidelines warn against eating too much salt. If your diet contains too much salt your blood pressure may become too high, which can cause heart and kidney disease. There are dietary values that are widely recognised as **recommended nutrient intake** (RNI); these recommendations are shown in Table 5.3.

Table 5.3 Recommended daily nutritional intakes

	Male	Female
Calories	2550 kcal	1940 kcal
Chloride	2500 mg	2500 mg
Copper	1.2 mg	1.2 mg
Folate	200 mg	200 mg
Iodine	140 mg	140 mg
Iron	8.7 mg	14.8 mg
Magnesium	300 mg	270 mg
Niacin	17 mg	13 mg
Phosphorus	550 mg	550 mg
Potassium	3.5 g	3.5 g
Protein	55.5 g	45 g
Selenium	75 mg	60 mg
Sodium	1.6 g	1.6 g
Vitamin A	700 mg	600 mg
Vitamin B	1.0 mg	0.8 mg
Vitamin B_1	1.0 mg	0.8 mg
Vitamin B_2	1.3 mg	1.1 mg
Vitamin B_6	1.4 mg	1.2 mg
Vitamin B_{12}	1.5 mg	1.5 mg
Vitamin C	40 mg	40 mg
Zinc	9.5 mg	7.0 mg

© Crown Copyright

5.3 Energy requirements

Whether you participate in sport or not, you need to eat enough for energy. The **basal metabolic rate** (**BMR**) is a measure of the amount of energy needed at rest. Food intake needs to take into account BMR in addition to the energy to participate in sport. Men can consume 2800–3000 kcal a day and women 2000–2200 kcal a day without putting on weight (Honeybourne *et al.*, 2000). Metabolic rates vary between individuals and get slower as a person ages.

Energy is measured in kilocalories and kilojoules – 1 kcal = 4.2 kJ.

Energy expenditure

Resting metabolic rate – average 60%
This is influenced by body composition, age, gender and genetic predisposition. Muscle is more active metabolically than fat, therefore an increase in muscle mass results in an increase in the resting metabolic rate (RMR).

Thermic effect of feeding – average 10%
This is due to the effects of digestion, absorption and metabolism of food. It is largely influenced by the calorie content of food, especially the ratio of

Figure 5.6

fat and carbohydrate. It is easier for the body to take on body fat from fat in the diet than it is to take on body fat from carbohydrates.

Thermic effect of activity – average 20%

This is the energy that is expended in addition but this varies more than the others. The thermic effect of activity is far higher for active people than for sedentary people. This has implications for those who participate in sport. The energy expenditure also depends on the type of activity and the duration of the activity.

Adaptive thermogenesis – average 10%

This energy expenditure is as a result of changes in temperature and physiological stresses. The body may respond by shivering.

Summary of the factors that affect energy expenditure

- Frequency of exercise.
- Intensity of exercise.
- Type and duration of exercise.
- Age, gender, body composition of individual.
- Fuels available.

In practice

Fuels available

- Protein is used during prolonged exercise.
- Alcohol cannot be metabolised by working muscles.
- Glycogen stored in the liver is used to top up glucose levels in the blood.
- Glycogen in the muscles from fat and carbohydrates.
- Water.

Figure 5.7 Dehydration must be avoided as much as possible

The intensity of exercise dictates the use of energy by the muscles. This energy needs to be replaced; without it the muscles would not be able to continue to function and the exercise would have to terminate.

Muscle cells burn carbohydrates and fatty acids when oxygen is present to produce **adenosine triphosphate** (**ATP**), which is essential for the muscles to contract. This process is called **aerobic metabolism** because it needs oxygen to proceed.

Part of the process can take place without oxygen, using only carbohydrate. This is called **anaerobic metabolism**.

The higher the intensity of exercise the more fuel consumed (in carbohydrates). If the intensity is approximately 50% of VO_2 max, then the fuel that is mainly used is fat. As soon as the intensity is raised to 75% of VO_2 max, then carbohydrate is the major fuel source.

5.4 Nutritional strategies in sport

Glycogen stores

It is essential that glycogen supplies are adequate for optimum energy supply. One method of increasing the glycogen available is through 'carbo-loading'. The sportsperson depletes his or her stores of glycogen by cutting down on carbohydrates and keeping to a diet of protein and fat for three days. Light training follows, with a high-carbohydrate diet for the three days leading up to the event. This has been shown to significantly increase the stores of glycogen and helps to offset fatigue. When an athlete is carbo-loading the diet should consist mainly of foods like pasta, bread, rice and fruit. Generally a high-carbohydrate diet will ensure that glycogen will be replenished during exercise.

Other energy-giving strategies

- Consume carbohydrates two to four hours before exercise.
- Consume a small amount of carbohydrates within the first half hour of exercise to ensure refuelling of glycogen.
- Eat carbohydrates straight after exercise for up to two days to replenish stores.

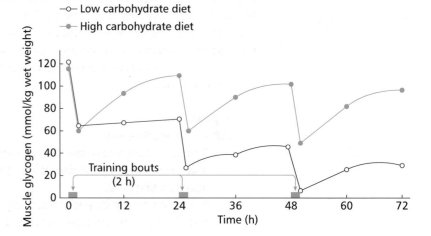

Figure 5.8 Levels of muscle glycogen over a period of time for high and low carbohydrate diets

Fluids

An athlete may lose up to one litre of water per hour during endurance exercise; therefore rehydration is essential, especially if environmental conditions are hot. By the time you become thirsty you are already dehydrated, so an athlete needs to drink plenty during and after exercise even if he or she experiences little thirst.

▌▌ *In practice*
Taking fluids
- *Take fluids, preferably water, before exercise to ensure full hydration.*
- *Take fluids continually during exercise, even if not thirsty.*
- *Small amounts, often, are best.*
- *Take fluids straight after exercise – and especially before consuming alcohol.*
- *Some sports-specific drinks may be useful for high-intensity and long-duration exercise.*

Figure 5.9 Take fluid regularly during exercise

Figure 5.10

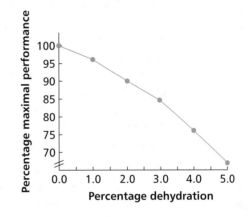

Vitamin and mineral supplements

There is an increase in the body's requirements for vitamins and minerals if regular, intensive exercise takes place. An athlete will need to eat more food because of the need for more energy. This in itself will mean that the body is receiving more vitamins and minerals. However, large quantities of extra vitamins and minerals can damage health, so care should be taken to monitor intakes. In certain circumstances supplementing the athlete's diet can be beneficial.

▌▌ *In practice*
Vitamin supplements
- *Smokers should consider taking extra vitamin C.*
- *A woman who is planning to become pregnant should take folic acid supplements.*
- *If you are on a diet and consuming less than 1200 calories per day supplements in low doses have been found to be beneficial.*

- *Vegans or vegetarians on a limited diet should consider multi-vitamins and mineral supplements.*

Supplementation is best considered under medical supervision.

Factors to consider with sports performers and nutrition

Sports performers, especially at the top level, have certain aspects to their lifestyles that should be considered when planning nutritional intake.

- Meals need to be timed to fit around training and competition.
- The diet must be well balanced.
- Fluid intake should be adequate.
- Iron intake should be adequate.
- Diet should be suitable for very high workload, depending on the activity.
- Psychological well-being is important. If an athlete is unhappy with the diet, then even if physiologically beneficial, it could negatively affect performance because of psychological pressure.
- Coach/dietician and performer should work together to agree the best strategy, depending on an individual's needs and perceptions.
- Obsession with food is common in high-performance athletes and should be avoided.

In practice

The diet of Mark Foster – Olympic and Commonwealth Games sprint swimmer

'I weigh about 14 stone, but when it comes to competition, I aim to have lost half a stone. I eat a lot of protein food. Two hours of work in the gym burns off anything, but while I watch my diet, I have a lot of protein drinks after weight sessions and take supplements to make sure my body does not become broken down.'

(Adapted from the Sunday Times *22 September 2002*)

5.5 Nutrition and weight management

Energy balance is realised when input (that is, food eaten) equals output (energy expended). When input exceeds output, the excess energy is stored as fat. The simple way to lose weight is to eat less and exercise more. However, problems can occur if energy intake is restricted over a long period of time or exercise is excessive, so it is necessary to reach a healthy balance. If too little energy is taken in, the body will lose other tissues as well as fat (particularly muscle) and this can slow down the way in which the body burns up stores of fat – therefore 'dieting' could result in more fat instead of less! In sport ready availability of energy is very important, and so the correct energy input must be maintained.

Body mass index

Your body mass index (BMI) is calculated from your height and weight:

$$BMI = \frac{\text{weight (in kilograms)}}{\text{height (in metres) squared}}$$

Definition

Diabetes

Diabetes is caused by a complete lack of insulin or a reduction of insulin production in the body. The hormone insulin, produced by the pancreas, is used to control blood glucose. With little or no insulin to trigger the breakdown of sugar, the cells cannot use glucose. There is consequently a rise in blood sugar, which becomes dangerous if not treated.

A BMI greater than 25 indicates that you are overweight. If it exceeds 35, then there is a severe health risk. A BMI over 30 for adults indicates **obesity**.

The incidence of obesity has doubled since 1990, and it is now recognised as a disease. Half the adult population of the UK is overweight. Obesity brings long-term health risks such as **diabetes**, infertility, pregnancy problems, back and knee problems, high cholesterol, heart disease, depression and low self-esteem.

In 2000, the British Heart Foundation reported that about 20% of four-year-old children in the UK are overweight and 8% are obese. In England the frequency of obesity increases throughout childhood, with 17% of 15 year olds officially obese. In the past 10 years the numbers of obese six year olds have doubled and of obese 15 year olds tripled. The first case of type-2 diabetes – a condition associated with obesity and previously found only in adults – has been confirmed in children living in the south-west.

BMI indicators:

- Less than 20 – underweight
- 20–24.9 – healthy weight
- 25–29.9 – overweight
- 30–40 – moderately obese
- 40+ – severely obese.

The BMI does not take into account body composition, which means that someone with a high percentage of lean body tissue may well weigh the same as (or more than) someone else with a similar (high) percentage of body fat – and obviously the two people would not be equally obese. The measurement of body fat is more accurate. Such techniques as skin-fold callipers or underwater weighing can be used to do this.

Preventing obesity

What happens in the home is crucial – parents have much influence on the lifestyles of their children. Did you know that someone watching television uses up less energy than just sitting doing nothing because the body is in such a relaxed state? Schools need to make sport and exercise an attractive way for pupils to spend their leisure time but if parents are inactive teachers have an uphill struggle! If parents are more motivated, then their children are more likely to follow.

Eating can be an enjoyable, social experience but if food is used to reinforce good behaviour too often it assumes too much importance. Attitudes are also copied from adults. For instance, if a parent diets even very young children pick up on this and express concern over their diets.

In practice

Preventing obesity in young people

- *Show positive role models in sport.*
- *Encourage and praise an active lifestyle.*
- *Get involved in active sport.*

- *Encourage the eating of a variety of foods.*
- *Eat as a family.*
- *Avoid controlling behaviour over food.*
- *Avoid critical comments about body weight.*

5.6 Issues related to nutrition and weight management

Lifestyle

Your weight is influenced heavily by your lifestyle, although much depends on your body type, age and genetic make-up. However, your lifestyle is something that you have some control over. The balance between energy intake and output is crucial. If your energy consumption is just enough for the needs of your body, then your weight will remain fairly constant.

During exercise your consumption of energy increases, and stays high for some time after you exercise. Exercising increases your metabolic rate and the calories that you have stored will be used. Aerobic exercise, such as swimming, running and cycling, is most effective at burning off body fat. It has been calculated that an average adult must walk more than 30 miles to burn up 3500 calories, which is the equivalent of 450 g of fat.

Exercise can also cause you to gain weight – you develop muscle, which weighs more than fat; therefore body composition measurement is far more accurate as an indicator of body fat than BMI.

Table 5.4 Calories expended in 30 minutes, depending on activity

Activity	Men (175 lb)	Women (135 lb)
Cycling	334	258
Hatha yoga	167	129
Dancing (general)	188	145
Gardening	209	161
Basketball	334	258
Frisbee	125	97
Horse riding	167	129
Skating	292	225
Soccer	292	225
Tennis	292	225
Hiking	251	193
Walking	146	113
Canoeing	292	225
Swimming	334	258

From *The Sunday Times*, 22 September 2002

Eating disorders

The eating disorders **anorexia** and **bulimia nervosa** are often triggered by life events. Sufferers use excessive slimming and exercising as a way of showing that they can control their bodies.

Anorexia nervosa

People who have an intense fear of becoming fat can develop anorexia nervosa, a condition in which a person will virtually starve herself (most sufferers are female), but they will often deny having a problem if asked. Even if the individual is underweight she will see herself as fat. Body weight is reduced by at least 15% below their average expected weight. Sufferers often have very low self-esteem and will often 'binge' eat and then vomit or may use laxatives extensively. Sufferers often withdraw from social contact and are obsessive in their manner; they can be depressed and anxious.

The health consequences of anorexia nervosa are severe, with gastrointestinal problems and increased risk of infection being common. Sports performers with anorexia nervosa find their performance levels and aerobic capacity fall. Approximately 10% of sufferers die. Early intervention is crucial if anorexia nervosa is to be overcome, but unfortunately one behavioural aspect of it is secrecy and the individual may well deny that she has problems.

In practice

A recent study by the British Medical Association has found that many models and actresses who are common role models for young girls have 10–15% fat, whereas the average for women is 22–26%.

One in six girls in the UK aged 15–18 years are dieting to lose weight and are likely to have poor intakes of vitamins and minerals, which are essential at this stage of life.

Bulimia nervosa

This eating disorder involves 'binge' eating then vomiting or using laxatives to get rid of the unwanted food. Sufferers may exercise excessively. A key feature is low self-esteem. In women excessively low weight causes menstrual problems, dehydration and cardiovascular problems.

In practice

Telephone helpline for eating disorders:
01603 621414

Coronary heart disease

Coronary heart disease (CHD) is a common cause of ill health and premature death. Approximately 1.4 million people in the UK are affected by it. Cholesterol can accumulate and oxidise in the walls of blood vessels, causing them to 'fur' and narrow (this is called arteriosclerosis). This reduces flow of blood to the heart, which can cause angina (chest pain), especially

---

Definition

Cholesterol

This is a type of fat that is actually essential to a healthy life. It is produced by the liver and taken in in the diet. Cholesterol is carried around the body in the blood attached to lipoproteins, which come in two forms – 'good' LDL (low-density lipoprotein) and 'bad' HDL (high-density lipoprotein). HDL-carrying cholesterol is 'bad' because it causes the accumulation of cholesterol in the vessel walls; the 'good' LDL transports the cholesterol back to the liver for disposal.

during exercise. Large blood clots can form in the vessel (**thrombosis**), stopping the blood flow to the heart.

Some of the major risk factors for CHD are uncontrollable – being male, age and having a family history of the disease. However, some risk factors can be controlled – smoking, high blood pressure, obesity and high blood cholesterol.

Controlling the risk of CHD:

- Eat a low-fat diet with plenty of fruit and vegetables.
- Lower alcohol consumption (maximum for males 3–4 units per day; females 2–3 units per day).
- Take plenty of physical exercise.
- Lower salt intake.
- Maintain a healthy body weight (BMI 20–25).
- Use only small amounts of unsaturated fat or cooking oil.
- Eat more fibre.
- Choose lean meat and poultry rather than fatty meat.

Slimming diets

Over 50% of people in the UK are overweight, and the medical profession strongly recommends that people eat properly and exercise regularly. There are many social and cultural pressures for being slim – for instance, fashion models are often excessively thin. However, frequent dieting can cause eating disorders and an unhealthy obsession with food.

There are no 'miracle' diets and dieting cannot control which area of the body weight is actually lost from. A sensible approach is to lose weight slowly, about 1 kg per week, and this may mean reducing the daily intake of calories by about 1000 kcal. Decreasing fat intake is most effective, and so is the reduction of alcohol intake – alcohol is high in energy. Eating plenty of fruit and vegetables will help to satisfy the appetite, as will eating starchy foods such as bread, rice and pasta.

In practice

Weight loss advice

The British Nutrition Foundation (2000) recommends that people should:

- *Exercise regularly.*
- *Cut down on fatty foods.*
- *Eat plenty of fruit, vegetables and starchy meals.*
- *Not skip meals.*
- *Follow nutritional guidelines for the population as a whole.*

Progress check

1 What do we mean by the following terms:
   (a) Food.
   (b) Nutrition.
   (c) Diet.
2 Give an example of each of the major components of food.
3 What are amino acids?
4 Why is water so valuable as part of a balanced diet?
5 **(a)** Name three different vitamins.
   (b) State why each should be part of your diet.
6 Why is food labelling so important?
7 What is meant by 'reduced fat' on foodstuffs?
8 Give four guidelines for healthy eating.
9 What is BMR?
10 What does carbo-loading mean?
11 Why is obesity so common in the western world?
12 What is meant by 'bad' cholesterol?

Psychology for sports performance

This chapter examines the psychological aspects of the individual and of teams in sports performance. The role of psychology in sport and the contribution of psychology to the enhancement of performance will be investigated and applied to sports situations.

Learning objectives

- To investigate the role of personality in sports performance.

- To investigate the importance of motivation in sports performance.

- To understand the nature of teamwork and factors that affect teamwork in sports performance.

- To investigate the nature of stress in sport.

- To examine the effects of stress and anxiety on sports performance.

- To investigate strategies that could be used to cope with the effects of stress and anxiety in sport.

Definition

Personality

'The sum total of an individual's characteristics that make him unique' – Hollander 1971.

'Personality represents those characteristics of the person that account for consistent patterns of behaviour' – Pervin 1993.

'The more or less stable and enduring organisation of a person's character, temperament, intellect and physique which determines the unique adjustment to the environment' – Eysenck 1969.

'Personality is an overall pattern of psychological characteristics that makes each person a unique individual' – Gill 1986.

6.1 Personality and sports performance

Personality and performance in sport has been a popular subject for sports psychologists, but hard evidence to back up theories on personality and sport is thin on the ground. Psychologists attempt to see links between certain types of people and success in sport. They also try to find links between types of **personality** and the sports they choose to become involved in. Most psychologists agree that there are two main theories that explain how our personalities are formed – the **trait theory** and the **social learning theory**.

Personality profiles

Sports psychologists have put in a great deal of time and effort to build a picture of typical personalities of sports performers. They have attempted to show that there are major differences between successful sportspeople and those that are unsuccessful or people who avoid sport altogether.

Morgan (1979) built on much previous research and found that many successful athletes had positive mental health characteristics. He investigated performers from a number of different sports using a questionnaire assessing the moods of sports performers – the Profile of Mood States (POMS). Successful athletes scored higher on positive moods and lower on negative moods (high-vigour and low-fatigue moods); unsuccessful athletes showed the opposite. However, these moods could be present because of the success of the athlete, rather than a predisposition. A graph of Morgan's results have an 'iceberg profile' (Figure 6.1).

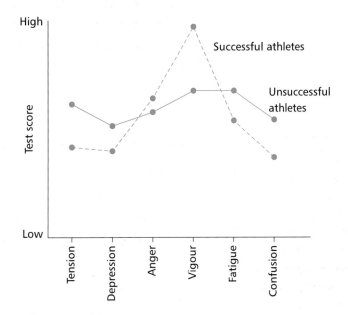

Figure 6.1 The iceberg profile

Sports that involve physical contact like wrestling attract people with a different group of personality characteristics than sports such as gymnastics (Kroll *et al.*, 1970). Team players have also been shown to be more anxious and extroverted but lack sensitivity and imagination associated with individual sports performers (Schurr *et al.*, 1977). There are also links between player positions and certain personality characteristics – for instance positions that depend on decision making, such as a midfield hockey player, are likely to be taken by a personality that has more concentration, anxiety control and confidence.

Trait theory of personality

The trait theory states that we have certain personality characteristics that we are born with and which influence the way in which we behave in all situations, whether in sport or in everyday life.

- Personality traits are **stable** – they vary little over time.
- They are also known to be **enduring** – therefore as individuals we are stuck with these characteristics.
- Psychologists have also found that traits are **generalisable** – Silva (1984) says that, according to the trait approach, our behaviour can be predicted in different situations and that there is always a predisposition to act in a particular way. Some sports performers for instance may have an aggressive trait, which may surface in a variety of different situations.

Figure 6.2 Type A individuals lack tolerance towards others!

Eysenck (1955) grouped the many personality characteristics into two dimensions or scales:

Extroversion ——————— Introversion

Stable ——————— Neurotic

Definition

Extrovert

Seeks social situations and likes excitement. Lacks concentration.

Introvert

Does not seek social situations, likes peace and quiet. Good at concentrating.

Stable

Does not swing from one emotion to another.

Neurotic

Highly anxious and has unpredictable emotions.

Each pair of traits should be viewed on a scale (or **continuum**) as shown. For instance, individuals may have elements of both extroversion and introversion but be slightly more extroverted than introverted.

There is another trait perspective to personality called the 'narrow band' approach. This states that personality characteristics can be grouped into two main types:

- **Type A** individuals are impatient and lack tolerance towards others. They also have high levels of personal anxiety.
- **Type B** people are far more relaxed and are more tolerant towards others. They have much lower personal anxiety.

Hinckle *et al.* (1989) researched the link between the narrow band approach and sports performance. In their trial 96 runners aged between 16 and 66 years were identified as either Type A or Type B personalities. There was no significant difference between the two groups, except Type A runners ran more when they were not motivated than did Type B. This research backs up the argument that no one particular personality type is preferable to another (Honeybourne *et al.*, 2000).

Personalities seem to vary during the lifetime of an individual, therefore the trait approach can be criticised as being too inflexible. Different situations often trigger off different personality characteristics: for instance a netball player may show signs of aggression only when losing.

Research has shown that there is a link between certain personality traits and the sports that are chosen for participation but there is little evidence to support the view that the trait approach can predict performance.

Social learning theory

The social learning approach states that our personalities are a group of characteristics that are learned rather than genetically predetermined. The situation is an important influence in this approach, which may account for sports performers' changes in behaviour rather than showing stable traits. Reactions to situations in sport are often based on how others have reacted in similar situations. According to this theory our behaviour is influenced by that of others, and we often copy or imitate others whose behaviour or personality we would like to emulate. People that influence us in this way are often referred to as 'significant others'. Sports stars therefore are more likely to be copied because their personalities and behaviour are seen as the 'ideal'.

▌*In practice*

A junior-school pupil who plays for the school team watches a Premier League football player being aggressive towards the referee. The boy will recognise the high status of the player and will wish to copy his behaviour. According to social learning theory, the boy will imitate the aggressive personality characteristic because of the significance of the football star to him as a role model.

It is important to remember that for every piece of research that makes a connection between one personality characteristic and a type of sport there is another which states the opposite. It is, however, important that we take into account the different feelings, concentration levels, motives and other personality characteristics of each individual when coaching. Only then will the coach be able to get the most out of the performers.

Personality tests have been used for selection of sports performers but it would be very dangerous to put much emphasis on this type of screening.

There are also research findings on the effects of sport on an individual's personality. It is common for claims to be made about sport being character building and that it can develop social qualities like teamwork that may be useful in everyday life and careers. Recent research has indicated that there is a link between sport and positive mental health (Gill 1986).

6.2 Motivation and sports performance

It is obviously important for sports performers to be well **motivated**, but some seem to be better motivated than others. The one who invariably wins appears to be better motivated.

Some people do not seem at all interested in participating in sport; others seem to be addicted to playing sport. If we could find out what actually motivates people to participate, we could encourage more to be involved in sport and thus enrich their lives.

Most psychologists agree that motivation is a driving force that encourages us to behave in a particular way. For example, an athlete may be

Figure 6.3 Intrinsic motivation is the internal drive to do well

driven to achieve a personal best in throwing the discus by the strong desire for self-fulfilment – to feel that she has challenged herself and has won.

Intrinsic motivation

Intrinsic motivation is the internal drive that people have to participate or to perform well. Intrinsic motives include fun, enjoyment and the satisfaction that is experienced by achieving something. Some athletes describe the intrinsic 'flow' experienced during competition. They speak of high levels of concentration and a feeling that they are in total control.

In practice

An occasional squash player who is 45 years of age reports that when he plays he often feels a sense of relief from the day's stresses and strains and that he enjoys the hard physical work of playing squash. This is a typical example of intrinsic motivation.

Extrinsic motivation

Extrinsic motivation involves influences external to the performer. For instance, the drive to do well in sport could come from the need to please others or to gain rewards like medals or badges – or in some cases large amounts of money. Rewards that include badges or prize money are referred to as **tangible rewards**. Rewards that involve getting first place in the league or getting praise from your parents are known as **intangible rewards**.

> ### Definition
>
> **Intrinsic motivation**
>
> 'Inner striving to be competent and self-determining; a sense of mastery over a task and to feel a sense of achievement' – Martens 1987.

Extrinsic motivation is very useful for encouraging better performance in sport. The reward acts as a **reinforcer**, which means that the actions that resulted in the reward are more likely to be repeated because the reward was so pleasurable. For instance, if a member of a karate club achieves a coloured belt for reaching a particular standard, the belt is a very obvious sign of that performer's standard and can be highly motivating.

Extrinsic motivation can increase levels of intrinsic motivation – this is called the **additive principle**. Some research findings, however, disagree and show that extrinsic reward can decrease the intrinsic motivation. For instance athletes' performances were shown to decline as soon as they had been signed up in contracts that paid a great deal of money.

▥ *In practice*
A young girl is just starting to learn to swim. After much effort she achieves a width of the pool without any help and without armbands. She is given a badge, which clearly shows everyone else that she has achieved success. This reward is pleasurable to the girl and her interest and determination in swimming increases. The reward has reinforced the correct behaviour.

Figure 6.4 In karate, coloured belts signify a particular level of expertise

---

Definition

Extrinsic motivation

The drive that is caused by motives that are external or environmental. These motives are rewards that can be tangible or intangible.

6.3 Achievement motivation

Personality characteristics and the intrinsic and extrinsic motives to participate and to achieve in sport are linked – the type of personality you have may determine how motivated you are.

Some people are motivated to succeed in sport, but others have personality characteristics that encourage them to avoid competition. Sports psychologists know personality characteristics related to motivation as **achievement motivation**.

Sport involves trying to achieve something, and this often leads to high levels of competition. If you set goals that stretch you as far as personal achievement is concerned, then your performance is likely to improve.

▥ *In practice*
A personal achievement goal for a basketball player might be to score 80% of baskets from the free throw line. This still might mean the team loses, but the player is motivated though personal achievement – and this may ultimately be a more powerful motivator to improve future performances.

Atkinson (1964) view achievement motivation as arising from personality trait characteristics (traits tend to be viewed as innate characteristics that we are born with). They grouped athletes into those that had a drive to succeed (need to achieve – Nach) and those who had a high fear of failure (need to avoid failure – Naf). They agreed that we all probably have both types of personality characteristics but some have more Nach characteristics than Naf characteristics and vice versa.

Definition

Need to achieve (Nach)

This is a personality type that involves the following characteristics:

- They persist on task.
- They complete the task quickly.
- They take risks.
- They take personal responsibility for their actions.
- They like feedback about their performance.

Need to avoid failure (Naf)

People with a Naf personality have the following characteristics:

- They give up on tasks easily.
- They take their time to complete the task.
- They avoid challenging situations.
- They do not take personal responsibility for their actions.
- They do not want feedback about results or performance.

Figure 6.5 Nach personality types persist on task and enjoy a challenge

If the performer and coach recognises the type of motive that drives the performer, they can devise strategies to improve performance.

In practice

To change a Naf into a Naf

- *Make sure that goals are challenging but achievable.*
- *Give early success.*
- *Show role models that have been successful.*
- *Be supportive and encouraging – give positive reinforcement.*
- *Use rewards.*
- *Seek to lower anxiety levels.*

6.4 Teamwork and groups

Groups are of particular interest to sports psychologists because in sport there are many situations where participants and spectators are in groups. The most common form of group in sport is the **team**. It is important for team members, coaches and supporters that a team works together well and all the individuals play as well as they can.

In practice

A volleyball team is a group because they share the goals of playing and to win and they have to interact by communicating with and responding to each other during game situations.

Team cohesion

For any team to be effective, the individuals in the team must work together well and share goals. If the reasons they are participating vary wildly, the

Definition

Group

A collection of individuals who share similar goals and who interact.

'A group is defined as two or more persons who are interacting with one another in such a manner that each person influences and is influenced by each other person.' – Shaw 1976.

'A collective identity, a sense of shared purpose or objectives, structured patterns of interaction, structured modes of communication, personal and/or task interdependence and interpersonal attraction.' – Carron 1980.

Definition

Team cohesion

'Cohesion concerns the motivational aspects, which attract individual members to the group and the resistance of those members to the group breaking up.' – Honeybourne et al 2000.

'The total field of forces, which act on members to remain in the group.' – Festinger et al 1963.

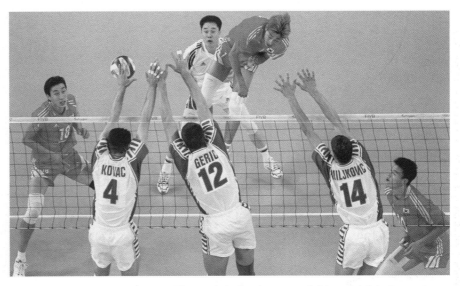

Figure 6.6 Good teamwork is essential in many sports

team is less likely to be cohesive. For instance, if half the team are playing to win more than anything else, but the other half are in it for the beer and curry, then clearly the team is likely to lack cohesion!

Factors that affect group or team cohesion

- How the individual members of the group feel about the group as a whole.
- Reasons for being attracted to the team – for social reasons or to be competitive.
- Group performance – if the team is winning then it is more likely to be cohesive.
- Support for the team – a supportive crowd will help cohesion.
- How well team members communicate.
- Leadership of the team – a good leader will improve team cohesion.
- Sense of identity – e.g. all players wearing the same kit.
- Friendship – if team members are friends outside the sporting environment, they are more likely to be a cohesive team.

Group performance

Individuals who are part of a group (or, in the sports context, a team) can play extremely well together one day, but badly the next. Some teams have many good players and yet cannot seem to play well together, whereas some teams have no individual 'stars' and yet are very successful. The performance of a team or group depends on a number of factors. If we investigate these factors, we are in a better position to get the most out of our teams.

Figure 6.7 Successful teams involve a high degree of cohesion

A psychologist called Steiner proposed a model in 1972, which can be useful when looking at the relationships between the individuals in a group and group performance.

**Actual productivity =
Potential productivity – Losses due to faulty process**

- Actual productivity is how the team finally performs – how well they play and their results.
- Potential productivity refers to the group's best possible performance. It involves the resources available and the individual abilities of the group members.
- Losses due to faulty processes means the problems that get in the way of the group reaching their potential. These faulty processes are mainly:
  - **Coordination faults**. These can arise from team members not connecting their play and poor interaction between team members.
  - **Motivation faults**. These can arise from individuals not trying very hard in the team, although others are trying hard to succeed as a team player. Lack of motivation of some players can prevent the team reaching its potential and becomes a faulty process, as indicated in Steiner's model.

Figure 6.8 Teams do not always play to their potential

▌▌▌*In practice*

In a rugby team there are a few players who do not seem to be trying very hard. When they get the ball, they 'do their own thing' and invariably lose the ball and valuable territory. One player in particular seems to 'disappear' for long intervals in the game and does not make himself available for the ball. This limits the options for the team in attacking play.

Figure 6.9 'Social loafing' can affect team performance

Social loafing and the Ringelmann effect

Social loafing is a term used to describe the behaviour of players who seem to lack motivation in team situations. 'Social loafers' do not try hard to achieve; they seem to be afraid of failure. These players lack confidence and are generally highly anxious. Psychologists recognise that such players may well lack identity within the team and therefore lack accountability – in other words, they can get away with doing little because no one will challenge them. This is not necessarily down to laziness; often the player does not want to let the team down, or feels unable to make any useful contribution to the team.

The Ringelmann effect is a phenomenon that may explain social loafing. It is social loafing-type behaviour that occurs when individual performance decreases with increase in group size. Ringelmann, an agricultural worker in the late-nineteenth century, found that in rope-pulling tasks, groups pulled with more force than an individual, but not with as much force as each individual pulling force put together – eight people did not pull eight times as hard as one individual, only four times as hard.

Figure 6.10

III *In practice*

Sports psychology research (Latane et al., 1980) involved a 'mock' relay swimming competition. The whole environment was designed to be as realistic as possible, with trophies, spectators, etc. If lap times were announced, competitors swam more quickly than if the lap times were not announced. The competitors' behaviour illustrates the Ringelmann effect – as individuals they lost their accountability within the team; they saw that their performance was unmonitored and therefore they did not need to try as hard.

Since social loafing is a feature of behaviour that is dysfunctional to team performance, coaches and players need to limit the Ringelmann effect. Strategies that could be used include:

- Giving individual feedback, rather than just team feedback.
- Ensuring that individuals have their own role in the team.
- Making all team members aware of the responsibilities that each team member holds.
- Positive reinforcement – e.g. giving praise to encourage reluctant performers.
- Monitoring performance of team members – e.g. via videotape.

III *In practice*

A netball player's coach videos a match, and goes through the player's individual performance with her. The coach highlights the positive aspects but also points out areas of weakness that could be worked upon for improvement.

Leadership

Leadership is a very important factor in team performance. Leaders influence behaviour in sport. There are many different leaders associated with sport, for example:

- captain
- manager
- director
- coach
- physiotherapist
- team sports psychologist.

Effective leaders influence the people around them, and in sport this can lead to better performances by individuals and teams. A good leader will also have clear goals and can motivate others to achieve these goals.

Qualities of a good leader

An effective leader has many qualities:

- Good communication skills.
- Enthusiasm and high level of motivation.
- Good sports skills.
- In-depth knowledge of the sport.

Definition

Leadership

'The behavioural process influencing individuals and groups towards set goals.' – Barrow 1977.

Figure 6.11 A good leader naturally commands respect

- Charisma – he or she naturally commands respect.
- A clear vision.

There is an ongoing debate about whether leaders are 'born or made' – are these characteristics innate or are they learned from others (social learning)? Most psychologists agree that it is probably a mixture of both. Some skills of communication and knowledge can be learned, but an outstanding leader is probably born with charismatic qualities that cannot be learned.

Leadership styles

The style that is adopted by a leader in sport depends on three factors:

1 The situation – e.g. is the team winning or losing?
2 The members of the team/group – e.g. are they hostile?
3 The personality of the leader – e.g. is he or she naturally forceful?

There are many different styles of leadership, but the three most common styles identified are:

- **Authoritarian style**, sometimes called task-oriented. This type of leader just wants to get the job or task done. They have no particular interest in personal relationships and they would make most of the decisions, rather than consulting other members of the team.
- **Democratic style**, sometimes known as person-oriented. These leaders are concerned with interpersonal relationships. The leader adopting this style would share out the decision-making and ask for advice from other group members.

Figure 6.12 A good leader has good communication skills

- **Laissez-faire style**. This type of leader takes very few decisions and gives little direction to the team. The group members choose what they would like to do and how they go about it, with little or no input from the leader.

In practice

Most successful coaches, captains, etc. have a mixture of styles to draw from. A good coach may decide to be authoritarian when the team are losing but more democratic in training. In match situations, he or she may decide to let the team 'get on with it' because interference might stifle creativity.

6.5 Stress and anxiety in sport

Much has been written about stress and its effect on sports performance. Competitors themselves are interested in why they are anxious in certain situations and not in others. Sportsmen and women participate because of the 'buzz' that they get from the activity. Excitement can be enjoyable, especially if you feel that you can cope with the demands of the activity. In sport, performers and coaches are particularly interested in how they cope with stressful situations.

> *. . . at the top . . . there is very little difference in the skill levels of the participants. It is thus the ability to handle arousal, anxiety and stress that separates the winner and the loser. – Jones 1990.*

Research indicates that it is the sports performer's perceptions of a situation that can cause **stress**. If a player thinks that they cannot cope with a situation (e.g. the final of a big tournament) he or she will experience the negative aspect of stress – **anxiety**.

Symptoms of stress

How do we know that a sport performer is feeling stressed? The definitions indicate that stress involves physiological and psychological symptoms.

Physiological symptoms
- Increased heart rate.
- Increased breathing rate.
- Increased blood pressure.
- Increase in adrenaline released.
- Perspiration increases.
- Blood sugar increase.

All these ensure that the body is ready for 'fight or flight'. In other words, the body is gearing up to cope with a dramatic increase in physical action.

Psychological symptoms
- Worry or apprehension.
- Irritability.
- Inability to concentrate.

Definition

Stress

'Stress is a pattern of negative physiological states and psychological responses occurring in situations where people perceive threats to their well-being which they may be unable to meet.' – Lazarus and Folkman 1984.

'. . . process whereby an individual perceives a threat and responds with a series of psychological and physiological changes including increased arousal and the experience of anxiety.' – Jarvis 1999.

Anxiety

'A negative emotional state caused by a situation that is seen as threatening.' – Woods 1998.

'Subjective feeling of apprehension and heightened physiological arousal.' – Levitt 1980.

- Difficulty in making decisions.
- Aggression.
- Increased rate of speech.

The psychological symptoms of stress are linked with the physiological symptoms. The increase in heart and breathing rates, for instance, can be recognised by the performer and this can make them worry and unable to concentrate on the task in hand.

Sources of stress

The factors that give sports performers stressful or anxious responses are called **stressors**. There are many stressors associated with participating.

- **Competition** is one of the most powerful stressors. Performers in sport are constantly being judged or evaluated by other players, coaches and spectators – and in some cases millions of people as a TV audience.
- **Frustration** can also be a stressor. Frustration can be caused by mistakes or the decisions of referees and other officials. Injury can be psychologically stressful because of the frustration caused by not being able to play properly – or at all.
- **Conflict** is also a serious stressor. There may be conflict with other players, coaches, managers or with the crowd.
- The **environment** can also be a stressor. The climate may be uncomfortably hot or the pitch surface unfamiliar and tricky to play on.

Figure 6.13 Extreme sport

In practice

A trampolinist in competition experiences high level of stress because, as she completes her compulsory routine, she perceives that she is being judged not only by the officials but also by other performers, who will be comparing her routine with their own efforts (competitive stressor). She is also aware that the trampoline bed is of a different tension from the one she has been used to (environmental stressor).

Eustress

Stress can help the sports performer, and some performers seek stressful situations rather than avoiding them. When an athlete experiences what is commonly known as **eustress**, he or she is well motivated and sees potentially dangerous or embarrassing situations as challenges. Eustress can enhance rather than hinder the performance in such situations.

In practice

A climber with a great deal of experience has confidence in his own ability. He continually seeks the 'ultimate challenge' and climbs in more and more difficult situations. He decides to climb without the support of a rope because he wants to experience the thrill of a potentially life-threatening activity. This is an example of eustress.

Figure 6.14 Some performers actively seek stressful situations

97

Definition

Trait anxiety (A Trait)

This is a personality trait that is enduring in the individual. A performer with high trait anxiety has the predisposition or the potential to react to situations with apprehension.

State anxiety (A State)

This is the anxiety in a particular situation. There are two types of state anxiety:

- Somatic – the body's response, e.g. tension, rapid pulse rate.
- Cognitive – the psychological worry over the situation.

Figure 6.15 Stressful situations cause state anxiety

Anxiety

This is the negative aspect of stress as a response. Anxiety involves worry that failure might occur, and of course in sport failure is always a possibility because of its competitive nature. In sport winning sometimes assumes gigantic proportions. As Bill Shankly, the inspired manager of Liverpool Football Club, reportedly stated: 'Football is not like life and death, it is more important than that.'

Some competitors can cope with anxiety and are mainly calm but others, including many top performers, can become extremely anxious. The anxiety experienced in sports competition is often referred to as **competitive anxiety**.

Competitive anxiety

Many sports psychologists agree that there are four major factors related to competitive anxiety:

- The interaction between the person and the situation. Some sports performers will be anxious in match situations but not in training.
- Anxiety can be caused by a response that is to do with a personality trait – **trait anxiety** – or by a response to a specific situation – **state anxiety**.
- Anxiety levels may vary. Those with high A Trait are likely to become anxious in highly stressful situations but are not equally anxious in all stressful situations.
- Competition factors. The interaction between personality factors, trait anxiety and the situation will affect behaviour and may cause state anxiety.

Martens (1990) developed the Sport Competition Anxiety Test (SCAT) to try to identify performers who were likely to suffer from anxiety in competitive situations.

Sport Competition Anxiety Test (SCAT)

This is a self-report questionnaire to assess sport competition anxiety in sports participants and measure competitive trait anxiety. The test can help to predict how anxious a performer will be in future competitions (i.e. their state anxiety).

There is a high correlation between the results of the SCAT and state anxiety before competition, and therefore the SCAT test can be seen as valid in predicting competitive state anxiety (Gill, 1986).

In practice

A coach decides that she would like to find out more about her hockey team players. She is particularly concerned that she can help those in her team who are particularly anxious in competitive situations. She administers the SCAT test and uses the results as part of her analysis of individual players, which may influence team selection but will also be used by the coach to help players who are overly anxious in matches.

Competitive Trait Anxiety

'A tendency to perceive competitive situations as threatening and to respond to these situations with feelings of apprehension or tension.' – Martens 1977.

Arousal

A term used for the intensity of the drive that is experienced by an athlete when trying to achieve a goal. High arousal can lead to high levels of stress, both physiological and psychological.

Drive theory

High levels of stress are often caused by over-anxiety to do well. Motivation is important but if personal drive becomes too much then performance can suffer. Another term for the amount of motivational drive that a sports performer has is **arousal**.

Hull (1943) suggested the drive theory to describe the effects of arousal on behaviour. This theory sees the relationship between arousal and performance as being linear:

Performance = Arousal × Skill Level

In other words, the higher the arousal, the better the performance. The more emotionally driven you are to achieve a goal the more likely you are to succeed. According to Hull, behaviour that is learned is more likely to be repeated if the stakes are high. The diagram below illustrates drive theory:

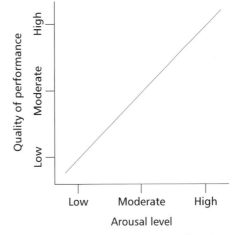

Figure 6.16 Drive theory

▌▌▌*In practice*

A weightlifter is well motivated to achieve his personal best. Just before he lifts, the coach is forceful with his encouragement, so much so that the performer gets angry and his arousal level is very high before he lifts. The 'psychological energy' that he has created is channelled into his lift and he achieves a personal best. This illustrates that the higher the arousal the better the performance.

The theory implies that the better a response is learned the more likely it is that high arousal will result in a better performance. The problem with this theory is that it does not always follow that a well-learned skill can always be performed correctly in situations of high pressure. The weightlifter in the example above may have gone to pieces and let his anger take him over, thus losing his technique. A boxer can never really lose his temper because this may cloud his judgement and affect his technique. It is also difficult to define what is meant by a 'well-learned task'. Many skills and combinations of skills in sport are a mixture of well-learned and novel tasks.

▌In practice

A Premiership football player steps up to take a penalty in the dying minutes of a crucial match. The player's arousal is very high because his performance will probably dictate whether his team wins or loses. He miss-hits the ball – an almost unheard-of response by this highly skilled player. On this occasion high levels of arousal lead to a poor performance.

Inverted U hypothesis

A generally more acceptable theory, but one that still has many problems associated with it, is the inverted U theory put forward by Yerkes and Dodson (1908). This theory has been applied to behaviour in sport. The theory states that as arousal increases, so does performance but only until moderate arousal levels are reached. As arousal gets even higher, then performance starts to decline. At very low levels and very high levels of arousal performance is therefore poor, but the optimum level of arousal for the best possible performance is at moderate level. The graph below illustrates this theory.

Figure 6.18 Moderate arousal will result in optimal performance

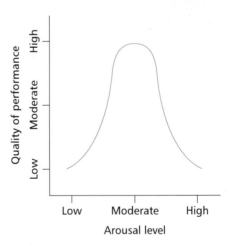

Figure 6.17 Inverted 'U' theory

▌In practice

A netball team player is well motivated and driven to win by her coach, but she keeps relatively calm and concentrates on the skills that she needs to perform. Her arousal level is at a moderate level and therefore she will play at her best. This is an example of the inverted U theory.

Research reveals that in sport the amount of arousal necessary depends on three factors:

- **Types of skill** – the more gross/simple the skill, the higher the levels of arousal are needed. When the skills needed are fine/complex, then lower levels of arousal are best.
- **Ability of the performer** – the more expert the performer, the more they need high levels of arousal to reach optimum performance.
- **Personality of the performer** – the more extrovert the performer then the more arousal they need to perform well. If the performer is introverted then arousal levels are best kept low.

6.6 Coping strategies

The management of stress to eliminate anxiety and to optimise performance is important, especially to high-level performers: 'The most important factors which separate the very best from the good is their ability to control anxiety at crucial moments' (Jones and Hardy, 1990).

Stress-management techniques are widely used by sportsmen and women to cope with high levels of anxiety. Increasingly sport has assumed huge importance – and not just to the performers.

Cognitive anxiety-management techniques affect the mind and therefore psychological anxiety. **Somatic** techniques, such as relaxation, affect the body directly. Cognitive techniques can affect somatic symptoms and vice versa. For example, controlling the heart rate by relaxation methods can make us feel more positive about performing; positive thinking can, in turn, control our heart rate (Honeybourne *et al.*, 2000).

The following stress-management techniques can be used as coping strategies.

Figure 6.19 Mental preparation is important to cope with stress

Imagery

Imagery can improve concentration and confidence. Imagery is the creation of pictures in our minds. Many players try to get the feeling of movement or to try and capture an emotional feeling.

▌*In practice*

A Winter Olympic athlete who is responsible for steering the team's bobsleigh visualises (uses imagery) to picture the track, with all its bends, twists and turns. He goes through the movements he has to perform when he pictures each aspect of the run in his mind. This is an example of imagery or mental rehearsal.

Imagery can also help with relaxation. A performer could, when he or she feels anxious, go to 'another place' in their minds to try to calm down. Many top performers report that they use this technique to lower their physiological and psychological arousal levels.

Figure 6.20

Figure 6.21

External imagery

This is when you can picture yourself from outside your body, like watching yourself on film. For example, a racing driver may go through the route in his mind before the race.

Internal imagery

This is when you imagine yourself doing the activity and can simulate the feelings of the activity, such as the bobsleigh example above or a high-jump athlete visualising the whole activity of run-up, jump and landing.

To be effective in using imagery the following points should be taken into consideration (Honeybourne *et al.*, 2000):

- Relax in a comfortable, warm setting before you attempt to practise imagery.
- If you want to improve skill by using imagery, then practise in a real-life situation.
- Imagery exercises should be short but frequent.
- Set goals for each session, e.g. concentrate on imagining the feel of a tennis serve in one short session.
- Construct a programme for your training in imagery.
- Evaluate your programme at regular intervals. Use the sports-imagery evaluation to help to assess your training.

Self talk

In this technique the sports performer is positive about past performances and future efforts by talking to him- or herself. This technique has been shown to help with self-confidence and to raise the levels of aspiration. Unfortunately, for many performers in sport self-talk can be negative. It is very common for sports performers to 'talk themselves out of winning' – for instance, a penalty taker saying to herself 'I will probably miss this'. This is known as **negative self-talk** and should be minimised if performance is to be good. High-level performers cannot afford to be negative and must develop strategies to change these negative thoughts into positive ones.

Martens (1990) identified five categories of negative thoughts:

1 Worry about performance – e.g. 'I think she is better than me.'
2 Inability to make decisions – e.g. 'Shall I pass, shall I hold, shall I shoot?'
3 Preoccupation with physical feelings – e.g. 'I feel too tired, I'm going to give up and rest.'
4 Thinking about what will happen if they lose – e.g. 'What will my coach say when I lose this point?'
5 Thoughts of not having the ability to do well – e.g. 'I am not good enough; he is better than me.'

Relaxation

Somatic anxiety can lead to cognitive anxiety, so the more physically relaxed you can get, the more mentally relaxed you can get. There is of course a happy medium in sport – you don't want to be too laid back because you need to react quickly and dynamically.

Figure 6.22
Positive thoughts are best!

Relaxation exercises before you attempt to train yourself in mental exercises such as imagery can be very useful. Relaxation helps the sportsperson to be calmer and steadier before performance. Relaxation skills are like any other type of skill, and you need to practise hard to achieve them.

Self-directed relaxation

Like other techniques this needs practice to be effective. In it muscle groups are relaxed one at a time, initially under the direction of the coach but when an athlete has mastered the technique he or she can do it without direct help. Eventually it will only take a very short time for full relaxation. This time factor is crucial if the athlete is to be able to use the strategy just before or during competition.

Progressive relaxation training

This is sometimes referred to as the Jacobsen technique, after its pioneer.

With this the athlete learns to be aware of the tension in the muscles and then releases all the tension. Because the athlete is so aware of the tension in the first place, they have a more effective sense of losing that tension when it goes.

Figure 6.23 Relaxation will help to manage stress

In practice

Using progressive relaxation training

- *Sit on the floor with your legs out straight in front of you.*
- *Now, tense the muscles of your right leg by pulling your toes up towards your knee using your leg and foot muscles.*
- *Develop as much tension as possible and hold for about five seconds. Concentrate on what it feels like.*
- *Now completely relax your leg muscles and let your foot go floppy. Concentrate on what the relaxed muscles feel like.*
- *Now try to relax your muscles even more.*
- *Your leg should feel far more relaxed.*

(adapted from Honeybourne et al., 2000)

In practice

David Hemery (who won an Olympic gold medal in 1968) described his relaxation technique:

'I lay on the bench and the others started jogging around, while I just stayed there, because that was what my plan was, trying to bring my pulse rate down. At will, I tend to be able to relax the whole body without going through the progressive bits.'

(adapted from Jones and Hardy 1990)

Goal setting

Goal setting is a useful strategy and one that is widely used in sport for training and performance. Goals tend to be more effective if they are set by coach and performer working together. Goal setting is a proven way of increasing motivation and confidence and controlling anxiety.

There are two types of goal that can be recognised and set in sport:

- **Performance goals** are related directly to the performance or technique of the activity.
- **Outcome goals** are concerned with the end result – whether you win or lose, for instance.

▌*In practice*

A tennis player is trying to improve his speed of serve by improving his timing – this is a performance goal. Another tennis player is trying to win the grand slam by winning each open tournament – this is an outcome goal.

Outcome goals tend to be more medium-to-long term and performance goals tend to be more short term.

There are four ways in which goals can affect performance (Lock and Latham, 1985):

1 They direct attention.
2 They control the amount of effort that is expended.
3 They improve the level of effort until the goal is reached.
4 They motivate to develop a variety of strategies/tactics to be successful.

Effective goal setting

For goal setting to be effective the overall goals must be broken down into achievable goals. For instance, to win the league, a team may have to concentrate on winning more games away from home. For this to be achieved, they may be set short-term goals of improving the attacking and/or defending skills. It can be more motivating to split long-term goals into medium-term and short-term goals, which are more specific and manageable over a short period of time.

▌*In practice*

SMARTER goal setting

S **Specific** *– if goals are clear and unambiguous they are more likely to be attained.*

M **Measurable** *– this is important for monitoring and makes you accountable.*

A **Agreed** *– the sharing of goal setting between coach and performer can give a sense of teamwork.*

R **Realistic** *– motivation will improve if goals can actually be reached.*

T **Timed** *– splitting up goals into short-term goals that are planned and progressive.*

E **Exciting** *– the more stimulating the activities can be the more motivating they will be.*

R **Recorded** *– crucial for monitoring progress. Once achieved, a goal can be deleted, thus improving motivation.*

Evaluation

Goals must be evaluated if progress is to be made and performance improved. Goals must therefore be clearly defined. This is easier with sports that involve objective measurements such as lap times – evaluation can only take place if goals are measurable. The measurement of goals will give information about success, in itself a motivating factor, and will also give useful information about the setting of further goals.

Sports performers need to know how they are progressing. Most are highly motivated and feedback is essential for them to maintain enthusiasm and commitment.

Progress check

1 Why are personality profiles important in sport?
2 Describe the POMS.
3 Give an example from sport to illustrate social learning theory.
4 Why is motivation important in sports performance?
5 What are the characteristics of a Nach personality?
6 Define a group or team.
7 What factors affect team cohesion in sport?
8 **(a)** What does social loafing mean?
   (b) How may social loafing be prevented in sport?
9 List four different leadership roles in sport.
10 What factors affect leadership styles?
11 Name three physiological and three psychological symptoms of stress.
12 What are the main stressors in sport?
13 Use examples from sport to describe coping strategies that could be used to combat stress.
14 How can goal setting be effective? Give examples from your own sport to illustrate your answer.

Training and fitness and fitness testing

This chapter covers the necessary information required by the BTEC specifications for the units on training and fitness testing. With the information contained in this chapter, students should be able to construct training programmes for different client groups. The chapter will cover the principles of training and how to apply them to training programmes. Long-term adaptations will be revisited from Chapter 4. Aspects of fitness testing and the importance of appropriate fitness tests will be discussed to help students construct and adapt training programmes.

Learning objectives

- To examine the principles of training.

- To apply principles of training to training programmes.

- To explore a variety of methods of fitness training.

- To examine the practice of fitness testing.

- To investigate the long-term adaptations of the body to fitness training.

7.1 Principles of training

Any training programme should take into account individual differences. An individual's goals must be understood – for instance, does the performer want to get generally fit or fit for a particular sport? The individual's current activity level must be assessed and initial fitness testing may be appropriate (more about fitness testing later in this chapter). The age, time available, equipment available and skill level must all be taken into consideration before the following principles of training are applied.

Specificity

The training undertaken should be specific and therefore relevant to the appropriate needs of the activity or the type of sport involved. For instance, *Figure 7.1* a sprinter would carry out plenty of anaerobic training because the event is

Figure 7.2 A sprinter would carry out plenty of anaerobic training

mostly anaerobic in nature. Muscle groups and actions involved in the training should be as specific as possible. There is, however, a general consensus that a good general fitness is required before any high degree of specificity can be applied.

Overload

The body should be worked harder than normal so that there is some stress and discomfort. Progress will follow overload because the body will respond by adapting to the stress experienced. For instance, in weight training the lifter will gradually attempt heavier weights or more repetitions, thus overloading the body.

Overload can be achieved by a combination of increasing the frequency, the intensity and the duration of the activity. These aspects are important if a **FITT** programme is to be followed.

Progression

Exercise should become progressively more difficult: once adaptations have occurred, then the performer should make even more demands on the body. However, it is important that progression does not mean 'overdoing it'. Training must be sensibly progressive and realistic if it is to be effective, otherwise injury could occur and there would be regression instead of progression.

Reversibility

Performance can regress, or deteriorate, if training stops or decreases in intensity for any length of time. If training is stopped, then the fitness gained will be largely lost. For instance, VO_2 max and muscle strength can decrease.

Definition

FITT

F Frequency of training (number of training sessions each week).

I Intensity of the exercise undertaken.

T Time or duration that the training takes up.

T Type of training to be considered that fulfils specific needs.

Figure 7.3

Variance

There should be variety in training methods. If training is too predictable, then performers can become de-motivated and bored. Overuse injuries are also common when training is too repetitive with one muscle group or part of the body, therefore variance can also help prevent injury.

7.2 Methods of fitness training

Warming up and cooling down

These are very important aspects of any training programme.

The warm up enables the body to prepare for the onset of exercise, decreasing the likelihood of injury and muscle soreness. It also releases adrenaline, which will start the process of speeding up the delivery of oxygen to the working muscles. An increase in muscle temperature will help to ensure that there is a ready supply of energy and that the muscle becomes more flexible to prevent injury.

The cool down is also important for effective training. If light exercise follows training, then oxygen can more effectively be flushed through the muscle tissue to oxidise lactic acid. Cooling down also prevents blood pooling in the veins, which can cause dizziness.

Figure 7.4 A warm-up decreases the likelihood of injury

Aerobic and anaerobic fitness training

Aerobic capacity can be improved through continuous, steady-state (sub-maximal) training. The rhythmic exercise of aerobics, continuous swimming or jogging are all good for aerobic fitness.

Definition

Karnoven Principle

This formula identifies correct training intensities as a percentage of the sum of the maximum heart rate reserve and resting heart rate. It is a valid measure because it takes into account the stress on the heart and the percentage of Vo_2 max of the athlete. The maximum heart rate reserve is calculated by subtracting an individual's resting heart rate from their maximum heart rate. The maximum heart rate can be calculated by subtracting age from 220.

It is suggested that the average athlete should work at a training intensity of 60–75% of maximal heart rate reserve.

This low-intensity exercise must take place over a long period of time, from 20 minutes to 2 hours. The intensity of this exercise should be 60–80% of your maximum heart rate. A widely recognised training formula is called the **Karnoven Principle.**

Anaerobic training involves high-intensity work that may be less frequent, although elite athletes will frequently train both aerobically and anaerobically.

Aerobic and anaerobic fitness-training methods

Interval training

This is one of the most popular types of training. It is adaptable to individual needs and sports. Interval training can improve both aerobic and anaerobic fitness. It is called interval training because there are intervals of work and intervals of rest.

- For training the aerobic system, there should be intervals of slower work, which is suitable for sports such as athletics and swimming and for team games such as hockey and football.
- For training the anaerobic system, there should be shorter intervals of more intense training.

The following factors should be taken into account before the design of a training session:

- **Duration of the work interval.** The work interval should be 3–10 seconds at high intensity for anaerobic and 7–8 minutes for aerobic exercise.
- **Speed (intensity) of the work interval.** Should be 90–100% of maximum intensity for anaerobic and moderate for aerobic exercise.
- **Number of repetitions.** This depends on the length of the work period. If the work period is short, then up to 50 repetitions is appropriate for anaerobic. For aerobic with a long work period, then 3–4 repetitions are more appropriate.
- **Number of sets of repetitions.** Repetitions can be divided into sets. For example, 50 repetitions could be divided into sets of five.
- **Duration of the rest interval.** The rest period is the length of time that the heart rate falls to about 150 bpm. Aerobic training will require a shorter rest interval for effective training.
- **Type of activity during the rest interval.** If the energy system is aerobic, then only light stretching is needed. For anaerobic activity then some light jogging may help to disperse lactic acid.

Fartlek training

This is also known as 'speed play'. Throughout the exercise, the speed and intensity of the training are varied. In a one-hour session, for instance, there may be walking activity (which is low in intensity) and very fast sprinting (which is high in intensity). This training is good for aerobic fitness because it is an endurance activity. It is good for anaerobic fitness because of the speed activities over a short period of time. Cross-country running with sprint activities every now and again is a simplistic but reasonable way of describing fartlek; it could also be incorporated into road running. Fartlek has the added benefit of a more varied and enjoyable way of endurance training. It helps to train both the aerobic and the anaerobic energy systems and is ideal for many team sports that include intermittent sprinting and long periods of moderate activity.

Muscular strength, muscular endurance and power training

For strength and power training, the performer needs to work against resistance. The training is effective only if it is specific enough. In other words the training needs to be targeted depending on the type of strength that needs to be developed, for instance explosive strength or strength endurance.

Circuit training

This involves a series of exercises that are arranged in a particular way called a circuit because the training involves repetition of each activity. The resistance that is used in circuits relates mainly to body weight and each exercise in the circuit is designed to work on a particular muscle group.

For effective training different muscle groups should be worked on at each station, with no two consecutive stations working the same muscle groups. For instance, an activity that uses the main muscle groups in the arms should be followed, by an exercise involving the muscle groups in the legs. The types of exercises that are involved in circuit training are press-ups, star jumps, dips and squat thrusts.

Circuit training can also incorporate skills in the activities. A circuit for footballers, for instance, may include dribbling activities, throw-ins, shuttle runs and shooting activities.

The duration and intensity depends on the types of activities incorporated. An example would be a circuit with one minute's worth of activity, followed by one minute's worth of rest. The whole circuit could then be repeated three times. Score at the end of the circuit may be related to time or repetitions and is a good way of motivating in training. It is also easy to see progression in fitness as more repetitions can be attempted or times improved as the weeks go by.

Weight and resistance training methods

In circuit training it is the body weight that is used as resistance to enable the body to work hard and to physiologically adapt to the training stresses. For strength to be developed more resistance can be used – in the form of weights or against other types of resistance, such as the use of pulleys.

Weight training involves a number of repetitions and sets, depending on the type of strength that needs to be developed. For throwing events in athletics, for example, training methods must involve very high resistance and low repetition. For strength endurance needed in swimming or cycling then more repetitions need to be involved, with lower resistance or lighter weights.

Figure 7.5

Figure 7.6 Weight training

Plyometrics

This type of training is designed to improve dynamic strength. Plyometrics improves the speed with which muscles contract. If muscles have previously been stretched, they tend to generate more force when contracted. Any sport that involves sprinting, throwing and jumping will benefit from this type of training, as will players of many team sports such as netball or rugby.

Plyometrics involves bounding, hopping and jumping, when muscles have to work concentrically (jumping up) and eccentrically (landing). One type of jumping used in this training method is called in-depth jumping, which is when the athlete jumps onto and off boxes. This type of training is very strenuous on the muscles and joints and a reasonable amount of fitness must be present before this training is attempted. As usual it is important that the muscles are warmed and stretched before attempting this type of training.

Flexibility training

This is sometimes called mobility training. It involves stretching exercises of the muscles, and can help with performance and avoid injury.

Active stretching

In active stretching the performer holds a contraction for 30–60 seconds. When the muscle is relaxed at the limit of the stretching range, muscle elongation may occur if this practice is repeated regularly. So the more you stretch the more flexible you will be! Ensure the stretching is under control and muscles are suitably warmed up before stretching begins.

One method of active stretching is **ballistic stretching**.

Figure 7.7 Ballistic stretching is useful for gymnasts

▌▌▌ *In practice*

Ballistic stretching

The subject actively uses the momentum of the limb to move it through a wider range. This is achieved through a bouncing-type movement. However, ballistic stretching should be attempted only by people who are extremely flexible (such as gymnasts or certain athletes) because it is easy to damage muscle tissues with such active stretching.

Passive stretching

In passive stretching an external 'helper' pushes or pulls the limb to stretch the appropriate muscles. This is obviously potentially dangerous, so the subject must be thoroughly warmed up and should go through some active stretching to begin with. Gymnasts often favour this particular type of stretching. One type of passive stretching is called **proprioceptive neuromuscular facilitation (PNF)**.

▥ *In practice*

PNF

This method tries to decrease the reflex shortening of the muscle being stretched, when the muscle is at its limit of stretch:

- *The limb is moved to its limit by the subject.*
- *It is then taken to the passive limit by a partner.*
- *Just before the point of real discomfort, the muscle is contracted isometrically for a few seconds, then relaxed.*
- *The muscle will then be able to be moved a little more during the next stretch.*

7.3 Constructing a fitness-training programme

Although individual needs will differ widely, there is an overall structure that all training programmes should follow. The principles of training outlined earlier in this chapter should be taken into consideration, as should the FITT principles.

Planning is crucial if any programme of training is to be effective. The programme should include training specific to out-of-season, just-before-season and during-season exercise. Training that is in phases like this is called **periodisation training**.

- **Off-season** (or out-of-season) training usually involves steady general conditioning to 'recharge the batteries' that have had heavy demands during the previous season.
- **Pre-season** training occurs over a period leading up to the beginning of the competitive season. Training is normally associated with endurance and high intensity.
- **During-season** training maintains fitness levels and involves achieving short-term goals to reach peak performance at a particular time of the year (e.g. an athlete preparing for the Olympics).

There are specific goals associated with these phases or periods, and these periods can themselves be split up into shorter-term goals. There are three recognised periods or units of time:

- Macro cycle – the number of weeks over the whole training period (e.g. 12 months).
- Meso cycle – a set number of weeks to attain short-term goals (e.g. eight weeks).
- Micro cycle – the short phase – usually one week, which is repeated up to the end of the meso cycle.

Honeybourne *et al.*, (2000) outline the essential components of any training programme:

- Identify the individual's training goal.
- Identify the macro, meso and micro cycles.
- Identify the fitness components to be improved.
- Establish the energy systems to be used.
- Identify the muscle groups that will be used.
- Evaluate the fitness components involved.

Table 7.1 Periodisation training for strength

Macro cycle	Meso cycle	Meso cycle	Meso cycle	Meso cycle	Meso cycle
Variable	Phase one: hypertrophy	Phase two: strength	Phase three: power	Phase four: peaking	Active rest
Sets	3–5	3–5	3–5	1–3	General activity
Repetitions	8–20	2–6	2–3	1–3	Or light resistance
Intensity	Low	High	High	Very high	Training
Duration	6 weeks	6 weeks	6 weeks	6 weeks	2 weeks

Amended from *Physiology of Sport and Exercise*, by JH Wilmore and DL Costill.

- Use a training diary.
- Vary the programme to maintain motivation.
- Include rest in the programme for recovery.
- Evaluate and reassess goals.

7.4 Fitness testing

Fitness tests, if done properly, can be useful in establishing the performer's strengths and weaknesses or areas for development. These tests can also be useful to monitor how well the fitness programme is working and how hard the performer is working. The results can be used to inform and update the next stage of the fitness programme. For example, if a performer shows low scores related to speed the training programme would be modified to incorporate much more speed work.

Fitness testing is often used as a screening device for selection to a particular team, for instance, because it may be indicative of that individual's potential.

Norms are provided with some of the tests given below, but it is important that individuals view the tests as benchmarks for their own improvements instead of norms, which notoriously rarely take into account all the variables present.

Reliability and validity will be visited in Chapter 11.

Strength tests

An objective measure of strength is a score on a dynamometer such as the **handgrip dynamometer,** which measures the strength of the handgrip.

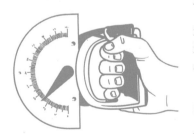

Figure 7.8 Grip dynamometer

▌In practice

Make sure that the handgrip is adjusted to fit the subject's hand. The subject should stand, holding the dynamometer parallel to the side of the body, with the dial facing away from the body. The handle should be squeezed as hard as possible without moving the arm. Three trials are recommended, with one minute's rest between each trial.

Table 7.2 Grip strength norms

Classification	Non-dominant hand (kg)	Dominant hand (kg)
Women		
Excellent	>37	>41
Good	34–36	38–40
Average	22–33	25–37
Poor	18–21	22–24
Very poor	<18	<22
Men		
Excellent	>68	>70
Good	56–67	62–69
Average	43–55	48–61
Poor	39–42	41–47
Very poor	<39	<41

For persons over 50 years of age reduce scores by 10%
Data from Wesson et al. (1998)

Speed

This can be measured by the **30 m sprint test** (on a flat non-slippery surface to prevent accidents). The sprinter should be timed from a flying start to the end of the 30 m stretch.

Table 7.3 Norms for the 30 m sprint test

Time (s)	Rating
Men	
<4.0	Excellent
4.2–4.0	Good
4.4–4.3	Average
4.6–4.5	Fair
>4.6	Poor
Women	
<4.5	Excellent
4.6–4.5	Good
4.8–4.7	Average
5.0–4.9	Fair
>5.0	Poor

From Wesson et al. (1998)

Figure 7.9 The 30m sprint test

Cardiovascular endurance

The level of endurance fitness is indicated by an individual's VO_2 max (the maximum amount of oxygen an individual can take in and use in one minute). The potential VO_2 max of an individual can be predicted using the **multistage fitness test** (sometimes called the 'beep' test). This test involves a shuttle run that gets progressively more difficult.

The test is published by the National Coaching Foundation (now sports coach UK) in the form of a cassette tape. Subjects are required to run a 20 m shuttle as many times as possible, ensuring that they turn at each end of the run in time with the 'beep' on the tape. The time between each beep on the tape is progressively reduced and so the shuttle run must be completed progressively faster. At the point when the subject cannot keep up with the bleeps, he or she is deemed to have reached their optimum level, which is recorded and used as a baseline for future tests or compared with national norms.

Muscular endurance

Testing the endurance of one particular muscle group can assess an individual's muscular endurance. One such test again comes from the National Coaching Foundation – the **abdominal conditioning test**. This tests the endurance of the abdominal muscle group by measuring the number of sit-ups (curl-ups) an individual can perform by again keeping to a 'beep'. When the individual cannot complete any more sit-ups in time with the beep, he or she has reached their optimum. Again this test can be used as a benchmark for training or used for comparison with national norms.

Flexibility

This can be tested using the **sit and reach test**. The subject sits on the floor with their legs outstretched. He or she reaches as far forward as possible, keeping their legs straight and in contact with the floor, and the distance that the ends of the fingers are from the feet (pointing upwards) is measured. Using a 'sit and reach' box ensures more accurate measurements. Once again this test can provide measurements that can be used in assessing any future training or for the subject to compare performance with national norms.

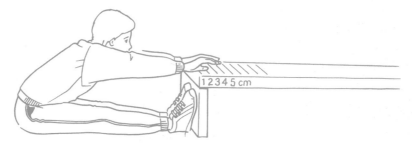

Figure 7.10 Sit and reach test

Figure 7.11

Power

Power can be assessed by using the **vertical jump test**. The subject jumps vertically, touches the calibrated scale on the board with one hand and the position of the touch is noted. The test is completed three times and the maximum height attained is recorded.

Anaerobic capacity

This can be tested by using the **Wingate anaerobic cycle test.** The subject warms up by cycling on the ergometer. When their heart rate reaches 150 bpm, an appropriate cycle workload is set on the ergometer (men 0.083–0.092 kg per kg of body weight; women 0.075 kg per kg of body weight). The subject then pedals as fast as possible for 30 seconds. The number of revolutions of the pedals is measured every five seconds and the power output at the end of the test calculated as:

$$\text{Output (watts)} = \text{Load (kg)} \times \text{Revolutions per 5 s} \times 11.765$$

This is a maximal test so it is important that the subject is fit and healthy enough to complete the test.

Body composition

This can be assessed in a number of different ways:

- **Skinfold measurement** – using a skinfold calliper. Measurements are taken from the biceps, triceps, subscapular and suprailiac areas. The total measurements are added together and compared with national norms (or, more importantly, to assess training or weight-management programmes).
- **Hydrostatic weighing** – measuring the water displaced when the subject is submerged in water.
- **Bioelectrical impedance** – a small electric current is passed through the body from the wrist to the ankle. Fat is known to restrict the flow of the electrical current, therefore the greater the current needed, the greater the percentage of body fat.

7.5 Long-term adaptations of the body to fitness training

Training is undertaken to improve fitness and skill levels. The capacity for the body to do extra work depends on how it adapts to cope with the stresses of the training undertaken. Long-term physiological adaptations follow after an extended and thorough training programme.

Aerobic adaptations

These follow an endurance-based training programme.

- The **structure of muscle fibres** will alter because of aerobic exercise, with **slow-twitch muscle fibre enlarging** to allow for more aerobic energy production.
- The **number of mitochondria increases**, as does their size. This gives greater potential for producing more aerobic energy.

- The **oxidative enzymes become more active**, which enables greater oxidation of the fuels of fat and glycogen.
- The **amount of myoglobin in muscle cells is increased** so more oxygen can be transported to the mitochondria.
- There is an **increase in capillarisation** around the muscle tissue; this improves the transport of oxygen to the muscles and carbon dioxide away from them.

Anaerobic adaptations

- Muscle cells increase in size, which is called **muscle hypertrophy**.
- There is an **increase in glycogen stores** in the muscle cells, especially following high-intensity training, which improves the ability of the muscle to break down glycogen in the absence of oxygen.
- The concentrations of **ATP and phosphocreatine increase,** which makes energy more readily available.
- **Tolerance to lactic acid increases** (often called buffering capacity), which enables the body to recover more quickly.

Oxygen transport system adaptations

- Increase in capillary density.
- Lowering of resting heart rate.
- Increase in vital capacity.
- Onset of fatigue delayed because of higher maximum oxygen uptake (VO_2 max).
- Size of heart increases – **cardiac hypertrophy.**
- Increase in stroke volume at rest and during exercise.
- Cardiac output increases.
- Decrease in resting blood pressure.
- Increase in numbers of red blood cells.
- Increase in haemoglobin levels in red blood cells.

Progress check

1. Name the main principles of training.
2. What is meant by the FITT principle?
3. Describe one fitness training method designed to improve aerobic fitness.
4. Explain what is meant by circuit training.
5. Describe why plyometrics affects muscle power.
6. Why is flexibility training so important?
7. Describe the process of periodisation related to creating a fitness programme.
8. Why are warm-ups and cool-downs so important?
9. Describe two different fitness tests and explain what it is that they test.
10. Describe the adaptation process that may occur in muscles after a training programme.

Principles of coaching

This chapter covers the necessary information required by the BTEC specifications for related units on principles of coaching. The roles, skills and qualities of the sports coach are covered, as are the types of knowledge and responsibilities. There is an examination of a range of coaching techniques used by sports coaches. Students will be able to apply theory to practice and therefore be able to plan, deliver and evaluate a sports coaching session.

Learning objectives

- To investigate the roles and responsibilities of sports coaches.

- To identify and examine the coaching techniques required to improve performance.

- To identify the factors that need to be taken into consideration when planning, delivering and evaluating coaching sessions.

8.1 Roles of a sports coach

Historically sport coaching has progressed as a position in parallel to the growth of competitive and professional sport. Coaches are mostly driven through need for achievement because their effectiveness will be assessed largely through results. Most sports coaches in the UK are unpaid and voluntary and consequently their employment status is low.

A sports coach has to adopt many roles to be effective and efficient:

- **Innovator** – The coach must often adopt the role of strategy maker. New and creative strategies may lead to innovation to individual and team performance.

- **Friend** – Coaches often find that performers trust them and close relationships form, which can develop into friendship. There are problems associated with this as far as objectivity and ethics are concerned: a coach must be careful to develop appropriate relationships and both teachers and coaches have found that sometimes 'familiarity can breed contempt'!

- **Manager** – A coach needs to be a good manager. Person-management skills are important to get the most out of the performers; financial

Figure 8.1 A coach must adopt many roles

management and management of equipment and facilities are also necessary. Some coaches have to book hotels and taxis and manage a whole host of other factors that are important in sports performance and events.

- **Trainer** – The coach often must adopt the role of trainer, either for physical fitness or for skill learning. Their instructions must be accurate and well informed and training programmes must be based on solid scientific knowledge. Coaches are at times asked to train other coaches, which is crucial if coach training is to be valid and relevant to the needs of the performers.
- **Educator** – The coach is often in the position of an educator rather than just an instructor and trainer. He or she may have to explain *why* activities and fitness sessions are important to the performer. Coaches often have to give advice about nutrition and general lifestyle. The coach often has the important role of educating the performer in ethical standards, morals and codes of behaviour, such as not taking performance-enhancing drugs, and reinforcing good practice.
- **Role model** – Coaches have a great responsibility, especially to young performers. People look up to them because of their status and therefore they are often copied and emulated. A coach's behaviour must always be of the highest professional and sporting standard so that performers, other coaches and spectators can follow their lead.

In practice
The coach's responsibility to promote appropriate codes of conduct

- *Provide participants and other people involved in the session with clear information on the ground rules for behaviour and the reasons for these rules.*

Figure 8.2 Coaches must give clear information

- *Encourage and reinforce behaviour that helps participants work well together and achieve the session's goals.*
- *Identify and respond to any behaviour likely to cause emotional distress or disruption to the session, in a way that is in line with accepted codes of conduct.*

8.2 Responsibilities of the coach

There are many responsibilities that come with the roles described above.
- There are legal obligations to take into consideration (see Chapter 2).
- The coach must show and reinforce professional conduct (see Chapter 2).
- It is important for coaches to protect the rights of children and abide by child protection policies (see Chapter 2).
- It is important for coaches to be appropriately insured. The governing body of each sport can often give advice about this so that the coach and the performer are protected.
- The coach has a big responsibility to ensure that he or she is well qualified for the activity that they are coaching.

In practice
Coach responsibility
The coach must assess and minimise risks during the coaching session:
- *Identify and take account of existing risk assessments for:*
  - *the activities you are planning*
  - *the resources you will be using.*

- *Check your plans and the environment in which the session will take place.*
- *Check the implications of any participants' special needs or medical conditions that may endanger themselves or others.*
- *Identify the likely hazards involved in the session and assess the risks of these hazards causing harm.*
- *Get advice from a competent person if there are hazards or risks you are not competent to identify and assess yourself.*
- *Plan how to minimise these risks to a level acceptable to national guidelines.*
- *Make sure you have information about the emergency procedures for the place where the session will take place.*

8.3 Skills needed for coaching

There are many skills associated with being a good coach.

Communication

It is important to communicate with performers, other coaches and officials if the coach is going to get the best out of everyone. Communication can be verbal and non-verbal, and effective communication includes listening, something that many coaches are not very good at!

▌▌*In practice*

Effective messages are ones that:
- *are **direct** – coherence and conciseness rule!*
- *are **consistent** – avoid double meanings.*
- ***separate fact from opinion** – be accurate in your analysis.*
- ***focus on one thing at a time** – too much information causes information overload.*
- ***repeat key points** – this reinforces and ensures no misunderstandings.*
- ***have a good 'sense of audience'** – adapt your content and technique depending on the recipient.*

Figure 8.3 A good coach is skilled at analysing performance

Organisation

An effective coach is well organised. Good organisation can relieve possible sources of stress and ultimately help performance. Confidence in the coach is increased if the performer perceives him or her to be organised. Self-confidence on the part of the coach can also be increased if personal organisation is good.

Analysing and problem solving

For effective strategies and tactics to be deployed there must be an analytical basis for decisions. If a coach is skilled at analysing what exactly is going wrong then it is more likely that the problem will be solved.

Education

Coaches also need to be able to educate those they coach regarding the following:

Nutrition

This includes:

- Hydration – types of hydration, reasons for hydration, hydration recommendations before during and after exercise.
- Food requirements for energy production – the role of carbohydrates, fats, protein and vitamins and minerals.
- Nutritional recommendations during exercise.

Sports psychology

- Basic goal-setting principles to include SMART, type and definitions of goal setting.
- Basic motivational principles to include what motivates people to exercise and the difference in motivating children and adults.
- The principles of anxiety and arousal including definitions of anxiety and arousal, signs of anxiety and arousal, anxiety and arousal management.
- The differences between novice, intermediate and advanced performers of skills.

Physiology

- The principles of warming up and cooling down.
- Fitness components – strength, speed, flexibility, power, agility and muscular endurance.
- The basic principles of strength, speed, power and endurance training.
- The basic energy supplies – aerobic energy and anaerobic energy.
- The types of flexibility and its role – injury prevention, improvement of performance.
- The principles of training – overload, progression, specificity, adaptation, variability, reversibility, recovery and over-training.

8.4 Coaching techniques

Depending on the situation, the coach should be able to incorporate a range of combinations of the following methods:

- **Whole, part, whole**. This is the technique of coaching a complete skill, splitting it up into parts and then teaching it as a whole again.
- **Shaping.** This is a technique in which reward or praise is given when the performer's behaviour/technique is correct. This **reinforces** the right technique, which is more likely to be repeated. The coach is therefore 'shaping' behaviour. This is sometimes called 'operant conditioning'.
- **Modelling.** This technique involves using demonstrations or 'models of performance'. The performer can readily see what is required and then attempt to copy it.

In practice
Reinforcement

- *Positive* reinforcement is the giving of a stimulus to ensure repetition of behaviour (e.g. badge for swimming).
- *Negative* reinforcement is taking away a stimulus to ensure that the correct behaviour is repeated (e.g. not giving any verbal praise if the performer uses the wrong movement).
- *Punishment* is giving a stimulus to prevent a behaviour occurring (e.g. dropping performer from the squad for not trying hard in training).

Teaching/coaching styles can be adapted to the situation, the performer and the coach themselves. Using the **command style (autocratic)** the coach makes all the decisions and directs the performer and is authoritarian in approach. The **reciprocal style** involves group work where performers learn from one another. When the coach takes a back seat and encourages the performer to discover solutions to problems he or she is using the **discovery style**. This approach by the coach may be termed **laissez-faire style**. The coach may adopt a **democratic style**, allowing performers to participate in decision making.

Individual participants prefer to learn in different ways: some learn better through instructions and demonstrations, for example; others prefer discovery learning/problem-solving experiences. Some prefer to learn through visual means, others more kinaesthetically.

The coach can adopt a variety of different guidance methods:

- **Visual** – e.g. demonstration.
- **Verbal** – e.g. instructions about technique.
- **Mechanical** – e.g. using a twisting belt in trampolining.
- **Manual** – e.g. supporting a gymnast for a handspring.
- **Feedback** given during or after the performance. Feedback is most effective if it is given close to the performance so the performance is fresh in the participant's mind. Feedback can motivate, change performance or reinforce learning. The more precise the feedback then the more beneficial it is.

Figure 8.4 Manual guidance

8.5 Planning and leading a coaching session

Initial planning

Coaching is fundamentally about providing a safe and ethical environment where a participant is able to maximise their potential within a sport or activity.

The participant must therefore be central to the coaching process. Thorough preparation based on the participant's needs is essential for the success of any coaching session. Coaches must also take account of guidelines from national governing bodies and their own experience when planning and preparing sessions.

Figure 8.5 Coaches use equipment to help in training

Coaches should take the following into consideration:

- Needs – including special/medical needs – and potential of the people taking part.
- Specific goals the participants should achieve.
- Coaching activities that will help them achieve these goals.
- Available equipment and facilities.
- Health and safety hazards and risks.

It is important for the coach who is planning the session to collect up-to-date information. He or she should then analyse the information and identify the implications for the coaching session and the participants. Throughout this process it is important that the coach maintains confidentiality where required and refers any participant whose needs and potential he or she cannot meet to someone else who is competent.

Specific information required by coaches

- How many participants are expected.
- Their physical/mental needs and potential.
- Any medical conditions.
- The aims of the programme of which the session is a part.
- The participants' preferred learning styles.
- Evaluations and action plans of other relevant sessions.

The coach should identify goals that meet the needs and potential of all the participants and should make sure the goals balance the needs of individuals and the group as a whole. Typical goals related to a session are to:

- improve physical ability
- improve mental ability
- improve skills and techniques
- provide fun and enjoyment.

Preparation of activities for the session

- Select activities and coaching styles that will motivate the participants to participate fully.
- Make sure that activities will enable all the different goals to be achieved.
- Plan realistic timings, sequences, intensity and duration of the activities.
- Strike an effective balance of coaching styles.
- Obtain the resources you need for the session.

▌▌▌*In practice*

Resources

- *The facilities for the session.*
- *Equipment for the session.*
- *Personal clothing and equipment.*
- *Any support needed from other staff.*

Delivery of the session

The coach should meet the participants punctually and make them feel welcome and at ease. The coach must then explain and agree the goals with the participants, making sure of their level of experience, ability and physical readiness to participate effectively and safely. It is very important that the coach ensures that the participants have the correct equipment and clothing.

The session must include an appropriate warm-up and an explanation of its value and purpose. The coach must be prepared to revise plans for the session if it is necessary. Flexibility is the sign of a good coach.

For coaching to be effective, explanations and demonstrations need to be technically correct and appropriate to the participants' needs and level of experience. Throughout the session the coach should check that the participants understand the activity.

8.6 Evaluating coaching sessions

Evaluation is the process of analysing the sessions you have planned and delivered. This can help to identify what went well and what could be improved.

Effective evaluation is essential if progress is to be made. Good coaches are always trying to improve what they do by thinking about and evaluating their coaching sessions, identifying strengths and weaknesses, and learning lessons for the future. The coach must also take into account developments in coaching practice and regularly study to develop their practice further and add to their coaching skills. This could include attending courses or conferences, reading journals or other relevant publications, and observing and working with other coaches.

When evaluating coaching it is important to review not just the way in which a session is delivered, but also the way it was planned. The key to really effective coaching is to plan well – a problem during a coaching session could well have been avoided if more thought had been put into the planning process.

It is also important to take into account how the participants felt about the coaching session via verbal feedback or a written evaluation. Their views are probably more objective than the coach's own views. Their comments may be affected by 'demand characteristics' (more in Chapter 11), when participants report what they think may please the reader, rather than the harsh truth!

It is important to record the self-evaluation of the coach, of other coaches and of the participants. However, the whole process is meaningless if these evaluations are not acted upon. The elements of the coaching that have received favourable evaluations should reinforce good practice and that practice should continue and develop. The issues that arise from poor evaluations should be addressed and become part of an **action plan** for improvement. Progress should be reviewed and there should be a development in coaching practice and updating of the personal action plans accordingly.

Progress check

1 Identify five roles that a coach has to perform in a sport of your choice.

2 Identify a brief code of conduct for a coach in your sport.

3 Using examples from sport, explain what responsibilities a coach might have.

4 When considering communication skills, what makes an effective message?

5 What aspects of sports psychology might be useful for a coach to consider?

6 **(a)** Explain what is meant by positive reinforcement.
   (b) How would you use it when coaching a beginner in sport?

7 When is the 'command style' of coaching appropriate in sport?

8 Use practical examples to explain what makes feedback effective.

9 What initial planning should a coach undertake for a successful coaching session?

10 How does a coach evaluate the effectiveness of a coaching session?

Sports development

This chapter covers the necessary information required by the BTEC specifications for units related to sports development. The chapter reviews the key concepts in sports development and the methods of organisations such as UK Sport to implement plans. The development of professional sporting structures will be reviewed along with their role in sports development in local authorities.

Learning objectives

- To identify and explain the concepts that are used in sports development.

- To explore the roles of local authorities in sports development.

- To identify and explain the role of other organisations in sports development.

- To evaluate the effectiveness of sports development.

9.1 Key concepts in sports development

The Sports Council, which was the precursor of UK Sport, saw the need for a coordinated response to sports development and produced a report called *Better Quality Sport for All* in 1996. In this report it highlighted the need to enable people to learn basic sports skills that could progress to sporting excellence. The strategy's aims were:

- To develop the skills and competence to enable sport to be enjoyed.
- For all to follow a lifestyle which includes active participation in sport and recreation.
- For people to achieve their personal goals at whatever their chosen level of involvement in sport.
- To develop excellence and to achieve success in sport at the highest level.

The strategy stated that everyone should have the right to play sport, whether it is for fun, for health, to enjoy the natural environment or to win.

Continuous improvement would help people to achieve their personal best, whether as participants, officials, administrators or high-level performers.

The challenge was to make 'England the sporting nation', and in response to this a **sport development continuum** was identified. There are several stages along the continuum.

Foundation

This refers to the work of local authorities in association with clubs and schools to develop basic movement and sports skills. The acquisition of good exercise habits with appropriate knowledge and understanding helps to develop a positive attitude to sports and physical activity.

The goals of this section of the continuum were:

- To increase curriculum time for PE.
- To increase the number of children taking part in extra-curricular sport.
- To increase the percentage of children taking part in out-of-school sport.
- To generate more positive attitudes to sport, especially by girls.
- To increase the percentage of young people taking part in a range of sports on a 'regular' basis.

Participation

This stage refers to creating as wide a participation level in sport as possible.

The goals of this section of the continuum were:

- To increase the number of people taking part in regular sporting activity.
- To reduce the drop-out in participation with age.
- To reduce barriers to participation.

Performance

This stage refers to the improvement of standards through coaching and training. It relates to competitive sport and encourages people to obtain fulfilment and enjoyment by improving their performance.

Goals of this section of the continuum:

- To increase the number of participants who are trying to improve their sporting skills.
- To increase the number of club members.

Excellence

This was about reaching the top standards in sport, for example national and international competition.

Goals of this section of the continuum:

- To achieve improved levels of performance in terms of world rankings, win–loss records, national and international records and individual personal bests.
- For English teams to achieve success in international competition.

Target groups

If sport development is to be effective and to be inclusive (in other words, to ensure that all sections of society are equally 'developed') target groups need to be identified and strategies put in place for each group. UK sports organisations have identified particular groups of people whose participation rates in sport are below those of other groups.

Definition

Sports equity

'This is concerned with fairness in sport, equality of access, recognizing inequalities and taking steps to address them. It is about changing the culture and structure of sport to ensure that it becomes equally accessible to all members of society, whatever their age, ability, gender, race, ethnicity, sexuality or social/economic status. Sports equity, then, is more concerned with the sport itself.' – Sport England 2002

Definition

Socialisation

This is a process of adopting the norms and values of your culture. It is about learning to be an accepted citizen. Appropriate behaviour is normally learned in the formative years from significant others such as parents.

Sport plays a major role in promoting the inclusion of all groups in society, although inequalities have always existed within sport. There is inequality in relation to gender, race and disability. These inequalities are largely a result of historical cultural influences – for example, male-dominated sports such as rugby were first played at public schools or in male-dominated environments, although an increasingly large number of women are now playing them. There are, however, still very few examples of female coaches at all levels in such sports.

The Macpherson Report of the Stephen Lawrence Inquiry, the success of UK Paralympians, high-profile campaigns such as 'Let's Kick Racism Out of Football', the Brighton Declaration on Women and Sport, and the evident multiculturalism of British society today all highlight the need for more equality of opportunity in sport, according to Sport England 2001.

The following are generally recognised as being under-represented groups in sport:

- ethnic minorities
- people with disabilities
- women
- people aged 50 and over.

These are not the only population groups that are under-represented. **Sports equity** concerns fairness and access for all. In sport, as in society in general, many individuals and groups may feel discriminated against.

The agreement of the government to fund sports authorities includes a commitment to ensure that the 'modernising' of sports governing bodies takes place. This includes how these bodies intend to ensure equal opportunities and a greater representation of minority groups in formal positions within the organisation.

Barriers to participation

All of us face barriers to participation but some individuals and groups have to overcome more obstacles than others.

The culture in the UK is diverse and we are proud to call ourselves multicultural, but in sport there are still examples and practices that move against the sense of sports equity described above.

▌In practice

'Let's Kick Racism out of Football'
This slogan was adopted by a campaign started in 1993 to cut racial harassment in football by fans and by players. The Commission for Racial Equality and the Professional Footballers Association both backed the campaign.

Sport is in many ways a reflection of our society, with norms and values that are historical and cultural. This process of **socialisation** can steer us towards certain sports – for instance girls towards netball and dance and boys towards football and wrestling. This makes sports equity very difficult because a boy who wants to be involved in ballet or a girl who wants to play rugby faces many social pressures to obstruct their participation.

Economic barriers also exist, with many sports seemingly out of reach for many people because they could not afford the equipment, facilities or membership fees. It may also be very difficult for people to afford the time away from work and family commitments to be involved in sport.

In Chapter 1 the barriers to participation are discussed in more detail.

9.2 Methods of development

Foundation and participation areas of the sport development continuum

- Ensure that images and photos used illustrate the range of participants currently involved in the sport.
- Governing-body publications to feature stories or articles that address the issue of equity within sport, from both positive and negative standpoints.
- Senior figures in the sport make public statements about their intention to tackle equity issues.
- Endorse an overall sports-equity statement, as well as specific equity policy statements for the priority groups (ethnic minority communities, disabled people and women).
- Allocate financial resources to equity planning.

For disability sport
- Promote the inclusion of disabled people in the mainstream programmes of national governing bodies of sport, local authorities and other providers.
- Increase funding.
- Raise the profile of sport for disabled people.

For women in sport
Statistics reveal a number of inequalities, particularly in the higher levels of coaching and administration. Female athletes made up 40% of the British team at the 1996 Olympic Games yet only 11% of coaches were women.

▌▌▌*In practice*

Gender equity

The Brighton Declaration on Women and Sport provided some principles to increase women's involvement and participation, including:

1 *Increase awareness of the issues surrounding women's and girls' involvement in sport.*
2 *Support women and girls to become involved in sport at all levels and in all capacities.*
3 *Encourage organisations to improve access to sporting opportunities for women and girls.*
4 *Challenge instances of inequality found in sport and seek to bring about change.*
5 *Raise the visibility of all British sportswomen.*

(British Sports Council 1994)

The Women's Sports Foundation (WSF) launched a framework in 1999, which states: 'The Action Plan aims to create a positive environment in which all women and girls have an equal opportunity and adequate resources to be involved in all areas of physical activity and sport at their chosen level.'

Other strategies:

- Provide gender-awareness training for governing-body coaches, leaders and organisers.
- Establish a programme of courses that will recruit women into the management of sport.
- Raise the profile of women in officiating.
- Provide financial support for top women athletes on a par with that of their male counterparts.

In practice

'Get Set Go!'

A personal development programme set up by the WSF in 2000, which helps women into sports leadership as coaches, administrators or officials. Governing bodies can identify women for these courses to encourage individuals in coaching and leadership roles.

For performance and excellence levels of the sport development continuum

There have been many initiatives by the government and organisations associated with sport, for instance Sport England and the Central Council of Physical Recreation (CCPR), to improve the levels of sports performance right from the basics all the way up to elite competitors. The following represent some of the important initiatives:

High Performance Coaching (HPC)

This is run by sports coach UK. If you are a coach working in or towards national and international level, you can use the resources and support from this initiative. Sports coach UK works in partnership with the UK Sports Institute (UKSI)/UKSport, home country sports councils, governing bodies, the British Olympic Association (BOA), British Association of Sport and Exercise Sciences (BASES) and National Sports Medicine Institute (NSMI). Its services include:

- CoachXL – an independent one-to-one needs analysis and personal development planning service for coaches.
- High performance coaching workshop programmes.

UK Sports Institutes

The UK Sports Institute is the name given to a network of centres and experts that supports the UK's top sportsmen and women. It is made up of four Home Country Sports Institutes (in England, Scotland, Wales and Northern Ireland) and a central services team, which is part of UK Sport, based in London.

The aim of the UK Sports Institute is to provide elite sportsmen and women with the support services and facilities they need to compete and win at the highest level. The services are provided locally, where athletes live, work and train.

The central services team provides a number of services directly to sports. These include the Athlete Medical Scheme, research and technical development, sports science, sports medicine, performance planning and guidance.

There is also IT advice, education and training. In addition, the central services team is responsible for the Athlete Career and Education (ACE UK) and World Class Coaching Programmes.

The English Institute of Sport consists of a network of training facilities and services for elite athletes, which is managed by nine regional institute boards.

A total of £120 million from the Sport England Lottery Fund is being spent on developing 80 facilities, including centres at the universities of Bath, Loughborough and East Anglia, and bases in Manchester, Sheffield, Gateshead, Lilleshall, Bisham Abbey, Holme Pierrepoint and London.

World Class Events Programme

This is an initiative of UK Sport. UK Sport has the lead role as the distributor of Lottery funds to bid for and stage major sporting events throughout the UK. The World Class Events Programme has supported over 70 events of World, European and Commonwealth status throughout the UK since 1997. Approximately £1.6 million of the total of £25 million of Lottery funding that UK Sport invests in World Class programmes each year is dedicated to the area of World Class major events in the UK.

The World Class Events Programme will generally support events only on a 'one-off' basis, except in very special circumstances. This ensures that money is not allocated to support the same event several times.

Sports Colleges

These are part of the government's initiative to recognise that certain schools have expertise in certain areas, such as languages, performing arts and sport. These 'specialist schools' develop links with outside agencies. Sports colleges must have an extensive extra-curricular programme, which includes links with external clubs. Sports colleges are dealt with in detail in Chapter 1.

9.3 Role of local authority sports development

Local authorities recognise the benefits of developing sport for their 'citizens'. They follow the national lead in developing sport to promote healthy living and the many social benefits of sport in creating a feeling of community. Sport plays an important part in raising self-esteem, and local authorities develop sport to ensure an overall better quality of life. Local authorities look at the participation trends in sport in their areas and target their resources and expertise to rectify apparent imbalances. This local approach under a national umbrella is aimed at inclusion, to try to include people in sport rather than to exclude them from participating.

Best value

This term refers to Sport England's initiative that underpins its Active Communities programme. The aim is to improve the provision of opportunities in sport for all the community. This aim was encouraged by government policy for modernising local government, which is set out in the 1998 White Paper *Modernising Local Government, in Touch with Local People*.

Best value was designed to make a positive impact on the means by which local authorities deliver sport to their local communities.

The 'four Cs' that Sport England sees as crucial for 'best value' are:
- challenge
- consult
- compare
- compete.

In practice

The value of sport

This highlights the key role of the public sector in enabling and providing sport at the local level. It actively champions the benefits and contribution that sport can make to the broader local authority policy agenda, including health, education, social inclusion, community safety, community regeneration, the economy and the environment.

(Sport England 1999)

Sports development methods

Local-authority sports-development policies and sports-development officers, who are experts in a particular sporting area as participants and coaches, use a variety of methods to promote and develop sport at all points of the sports development continuum. Local authorities will support local schools and colleges with help and advice from their sports development officers. Local authorities will also help local organisations in their development of sports facilities both with financial help and advice about strategy and building regulations. They will often run coaching education programmes for all levels of prospective coaches. To increase participation and interest in sport local authorities run 'taster sessions' in sports, summer schools, competitions and tournaments in a wide variety of sports.

These sports development methods are often targeted at the groups of people that are under-represented to encourage social inclusion.

In practice

Case study: Birmingham City Council sports development

Sports development officers are personally involved in providing daily and weekly sessions in a wide range of sports, delivering new opportunities and maintaining community sports activities around the city.

The City Council is committed to increasing opportunity for people from under-represented groups within the community. Women and girls, people from ethnic minority groups and people with disabilities are a focus at all levels of sports development work.

The City Council set out to increase participation and develop sporting skills and it recognises that this requires committed, well-trained coaches, teachers and instructors. They are involved in the organisation of a wide range of courses and seminars for coaches at all levels. Particular emphasis is placed on vocational qualifications through links with the governing bodies of sport, colleges and training agencies.

The City Council views sports development as working with others to form partnerships. It works with voluntary organisations and statutory bodies to develop sport and events of special interest for the people of Birmingham. There is a network of strong partnerships, working together with voluntary sporting organisations. Key partners include the Sports Council, the National Coaching Foundation (now sports coach UK), the Central Council for Physical Recreation, governing bodies of sport, the Birmingham Sports Advisory Council and several organisations within the business community of Birmingham.

The Sport Development Team has focused on the sports development continuum:

1 *Foundation. Work in association with clubs and schools developing sporting skills with primary school-age children. The acquisition of good exercise habits provides a basis for personal development and future participation in sport.*

2 *Participation. Sports clubs and other voluntary organisations are the essential partners in creating a wide participation level for all ages, if only for reasons of enjoyment, fitness or a simple desire to get involved in sport. The development of school–club links and the process of supporting community sports clubs with the help of leisure centre managers is an important part of the Council's strategy.*

3 *Performance. Coaching schemes are an essential part of the sports development in Birmingham, providing opportunities for participants to achieve their potential and obtain fulfilment and enjoyment from improving their performance. School holiday courses, weekly sessions and close links with local governing bodies of sport are a strong feature at this level.*

4 *Excellence. The Council runs sports development-led programmes – and, more particularly, has created partnerships to provide increased opportunities for participants of national and international calibre to emerge.*

9.4 Role and effectiveness of organisations

The role of many sports-related organisations (including sports coach UK, Youth Sports Trust, CCPR, sports councils, national governing bodies) has been detailed in Chapter 1. The following organisations are also involved in sports development:

National Association for Sports Development

This organisation provides support and professional development. Following a year's consultation with leading figures in the field, the National Association for Sports Development was formed with effect from 1 April 2000. In order to support its work, partnerships have been established with the Institute of Sport and Recreation Management (ISRM). The organisation is committed to raising the profile of sports development and sports development officers.

English Federation for Disability Sport (EFDS)

This is a national body that is responsible for developing sport for people with disabilities in England. It works closely with the other national disability organisations recognised by Sport England:
- British Amputees and Les Autres Sports Association
- British Blind Sport
- British Deaf Sports Council
- British Wheelchair Sports Foundation
- Cerebral Palsy Sport
- Disability Sport England
- English Sports Association for People with Learning Disability.

The EFDS has a four-year national plan, *Building a Fairer Sporting Society*, which outlines the inclusion of disabled people in the identified national priority sports of athletics, boccia, cricket, football, goalball and swimming. They are also involved in the development of coach education and training opportunities, which are accessible to disabled people and cover the technical issues of coaching disabled people.

The objectives of the EFDS are:
- The creation of programmes for grass-roots participation by disabled people.
- The delivery of a rationalised programme of championships and events for disabled people.
- The establishment of a talent identification system for disabled players and athletes.
- The establishment of regional and national training squads for disabled players and athletes.

Effectiveness of organisations

The criteria that many organisations use for assessing their effectiveness include:
- **Value for money** – a cost/benefit analysis based on financial and human resources. For this type of evaluation to take place, it is important that there are objective measures for both the costs and the rewards. The problem is that many 'rewards', e.g. participation rates, may not be obvious and may also have an effect in the long term rather than the short term.

- **Achievement of aims and objectives** – All sports organisations have stated aims and objectives, which are largely measurable. There is normally a short-, medium- and long-term assessment of these aims and objectives.
- **Consultation** – Feedback on performance is not necessarily about statistics related to success and participation rates. There can also be some very useful feedback from officers of the organisations and other partner agencies as well as the sports participants and the general public. This can take the form of a questionnaire and/or an interview. Many organisations hire a market research team to ensure that the gathering of the relevant information is valid and reliable.

In practice

Sport England evaluation strategies

The extension of the QUEST (quality accreditation and self-assessment) concepts to sports development was the subject of a feasibility study commissioned by Sport England. This identified that the development of a set of quality standards for service delivery in sports development was crucial to continuous improvement and self-assessment.

The Model Survey Package is a guidance manual produced by Sport England to assist local authorities in carrying out market research in their areas. The manual gives practical guidance on how to carry out statistically sound surveys of sports-facility customers, people using parks and other outdoor recreation sites, and household surveys.

Definition
QUEST The scheme, with origins in the British Quality Association Leisure Services Sub Committee, was launched in 1996, to set clear standards and encourage continuous improvement in sport and leisure activities.

Progress check

1 What is meant by the sport development continuum?
2 Give examples from sport to describe the participation stage of the sports development continuum.
3 What groups are targeted for sports development and why are they targeted?
4 Define sports equity.
5 **(a)** Describe some of the barriers that prevent participation in sport.
  (b) Give examples of how these barriers are being dismantled.
6 How is Disability Sport being developed?
7 What role do the UK sports institutes play in sports development?
8 Explain the term 'best value' used in Sport England's initiative.
9 Describe the sports development methods that are currently being used in the UK.
10 Describe the criteria for evaluating the effectiveness of sports organisations in sports development.

10 Skill learning and performance

This chapter covers the necessary information required by the BTEC specifications for units related to acquisition of motor skills and their performance. The chapter will explore the nature of skill and its classifications, and will explain how information related to skilled performance is processed and programmed. The principles that underpin skill learning and how that knowledge may be applied to make practice sessions more effective will be investigated.

Learning objectives

- To investigate and understand the nature of skilled performance.
- To explain the ways that sports performers process information in skilled performance.
- To investigate the concept of motor programmes.
- To apply the theoretical concepts to practical sessions.

Figure 10.1 Skilful movement is fluent and coordinated

10.1 The nature of skill and activity

Skill can be used to describe a movement like shooting a basketball, but often we use it to describe the overall actions of someone who is good at what they do. There are two main ways of using the word 'skill':

- As a specific task to be performed.
- To describe the quality of a particular action, which might include how consistent the performance is and how prepared the performer is to carry out the task.

When a professional footballer, for instance, performs a skilful pass, he shows a technically good movement but also the way in which he passes the ball has qualities that we might describe collectively as being 'skilful'. Qualities used to describe skilful movement include fluent, coordinated, controlled, goal-directed, efficient, consistent, technically accurate and aesthetically pleasing.

Skills are learned and involve pre-planned movements that are goal directed. To carry out skills, we need certain factors such as strength and good hand–eye coordination. These factors are known as abilities.

Figure 10.2

Abilities are different from skills because they are largely determined genetically – they are natural and enduring characteristics.

Classification of skills

For the nature of skills to be understood fully it is helpful to classify them. Classification clarifies what is required to learn and perform a particular skill.

If, for instance, you wish to coach a performer to shoot the ball in netball, it would be useful to know that the skill is not affected much by the environment and that the shooter has complete control over how the technique is executed. The coach can then train the shooter to shut out much of the external stimuli and to concentrate on a smooth and fluent technique.

If a skill is affected by the surrounding environment and requires the performer to make perceptual decisions, it is called an **open skill.** At the other extreme a skill that is not affected at all by the environment is called a **closed skill.**

▌*In practice*

Open/closed skills

An example of a skill that is open is a tackle in hockey – the player making the tackle has to take into account the position of the other player, the position of the ball and the speed of both. There are many perceptual requirements.

Figure 10.3

Definition

Cognitive skills

Skills that involve intellectual ability. These skills affect the perceptual process and help us to make sense of what is required in any given situation. They are essential if the performer is to make correct and effective decisions.

Psychomotor ability

The ability to process information regarding movement and then to put decisions into action. Psychomotor abilities include reaction time and limb coordination.

Gross motor ability

Ability involving actual movement – for example, strength, flexibility, speed.

Figure 10.4 A serial skill is the triple jump

An example of a skill that is closed would be a basketball free throw. The environment remains fairly constant. The basket is a set height, the distance away from the basket is also set and the player has no active opponent to interfere with their shot.

Skills can be classified according to their perceptual requirements, the types of judgements and decisions that a person has to make to perform the skill. If there are many decisions to make, the skill is known as a **complex skill** and may have to be learned in stages. If the skill is a straightforward one with hardly any judgements or decisions to make then it is known as a **simple skill** and can be taught as a whole and in a fairly repetitive way.

The type of skill and the way in which it is made up or organised can also be classified so that effective teaching and learning can take place.

- If a skill has elements or **sub-routines** that are very difficult to separate, then it is known as a **highly organised** skill. An example would be dribbling the ball in basketball.
- If a skill has sub-routines that are easily identified as separate movements then it has **low organisation.** A tennis serve is such a skill.

It is difficult to classify skills, because by their nature they are not easily put into separate categories. Classification also depends on the environment in which the skill is executed and the skill and ability levels of the performer. It is therefore accepted that classification must involve the use of a **continuum** or scale.

- Skills that have a definite beginning and end are called **discrete skills**, such as kicking a football.
- Some of these discrete skills may have some separate elements to them, which makes them more like **serial skills**, in other words a small collection of separate skills rolled into one (e.g. the triple jump in athletics).
- In other skills it is very difficult to separate out the sub-routines because the elements are highly organised. These are called **continuous skills**, and an example is the leg action in cycling.

In practice

The discrete – serial – continuous continuum

Discrete   1   2   Serial   3   Continuous

1 Skill such as shot put
2 Skill such as high jump
3 Skill such as flutter-kick leg action in swimming.

Implications for training and coaching

If a coach and a performer are familiar with and understand the nature of the task or skill that has to be learned and performed, then training techniques can be adapted depending on these requirements.

- Teaching a closed skill is more effective if the skill is practised repetitively so that the skill becomes 'grooved'. It is also unnecessary to vary the situation because in closed skills it remains mainly constant.

Definition

Kinaesthetic sense

This is the feeling or sense that we get through movement. Our proprioceptors (found in our muscles, ligaments and joints) pick up signals that feed back to the brain to tell us where we are and what we are doing. For example, the kinaesthetic sense of cycling with stabilisers will be different to the feelings that you get from muscles when you are cycling without mechanical help. Therefore it is important to get the 'true' sense of the skill as quickly as you can in skill learning.

Figure 10.5

- To teach an open skill a variety of situations would be effective, helping the performer to build up a repertoire of strategies to cope with the ever-changing circumstances.
- It is probably more effective to teach a discrete skill as a whole rather than artificially try to split it up into parts.
- In coaching a serial skill it would be more effective to teach and practise each element separately and then to string the sub-routines together and practise the skill as a whole.

It is difficult to split a continuous skill into sub-routines because the 'flow' of the skill may be disturbed. It is probably more effective to practise as a whole so that the **kinaesthetic sense** of the skill is not lost.

10.2 Information processing

The nature of the human mind and how it works is still mainly a mystery. In sport, skills are learned and performed by making decisions. Our brain has to take in information from the environment and draw on previous experiences before it sends messages to our muscles to move in particular ways. This whole process is not fully understood but one way that scientists and in particular psychologists have tried to explain the process is likening the brain to a machine or computer.

Just as information goes into a computer to be processed, stimuli enter the brain to be considered before action. This is called **sensory input.**

In practice

Input – catching a ball
The information that enters the brain includes the type of ball, the speed of the ball, the trajectory of the ball and the distance away from the source of the throw.

Figure 10.6

Figure 10.7 Catching a ball involves processing stimuli

When information enters the brain it is coded and sorted to recognise what the stimulus means. Part of this recognition comes from previous experiences and so our **memory** plays an important part in the processing of information. The more experienced a player, the more his or her memory can be drawn upon for future performances because they have performed successful and unsuccessful movements that can either be repeated or avoided. The process of sorting out information and making judgements about what it is and what it means is called **perception.**

▌▌▌ In practice
Memory

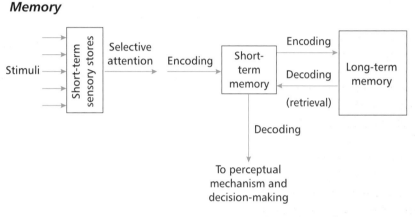

Figure 10.8 The memory process

*Information (stimuli) is filtered by the short-term sensory store – a process called **selective attention**. The stimuli that are selected pass through the short-term memory store and are organised into manageable 'chunks'. This information is then used by the perceptual mechanism, having been influenced by the information drawn from the long-term memory. Information can also be passed into the long-term memory if it is repeated and is important enough.*

Once the information has been through the perceptual mechanism, the brain has to formulate a plan regarding the movement that is to take place – the **decision-making mechanism.** If the performer is batting in a cricket match, and the ball has been bowled, the player has to decide which shot to play, based on the information that has been filtered and the influence of the memory – all in a split second.

Once the decision has been made the signals are passed through the nervous system to the muscles. This is called the **effector mechanism.** The muscles then move and the skill or groups of skills are performed.

As the performance takes place and after completion of the action, we receive information that tells us how well we have done and what to do next time. This process is called **feedback**. The coach must give feedback to the performer because he or she may not be able to detect errors on their own because of limited kinaesthetic sense. For example, a novice gymnast might not be aware of what a good handstand feels like and therefore feedback

Figure 10.9

related to the end result would help him or her detect errors. The coach could use a video of the performance to show the novice how he performed.

In practice

Feedback

Feedback involves using the information that is available to the performer during the performance of a skill or after the response to alter the performance. There are several forms of feedback:

- *Continuous feedback – feedback during the performance, in the form of kinaesthesis or proprioception.*
- *Terminal feedback – feedback after the response has been completed.*
- *Knowledge of results – a type of terminal feedback that gives the performer information about the end result.*
- *Knowledge of performance – information about how well the movement is being executed, rather than the end result.*
- *Internal/intrinsic feedback – a type of continuous feedback that comes from the proprioceptors.*
- *External/extrinsic/augmented feedback – feedback that comes from external sources, such as sound or vision.*
- *Positive feedback – reinforces skill learning and gives information about a successful outcome.*
- *Negative feedback – information that concerns something that has failed. This can ensure that the movement is not repeated and that other strategies can be deployed next time.*

Information processing model

The flow diagram below summarises the concept of information processing.

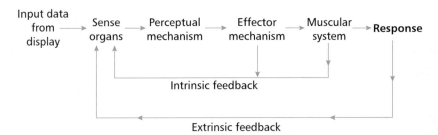

Figure 10.10 Information processing model

Reaction time

It is important in many sports situations that the performer has quick reactions, whether it is waiting for the starting pistol in 100 m sprint or timing a tackle in rugby. Various terms are used when considering reaction time: **reaction time**, **movement time**, **response time.**

Factors that affect the ability to react quickly:

- The number of choices that have to be made – the more choices, the longer it takes to react. This is illustrated in **Hick's Law**. If there is only

Definition

Single-channel hypothesis

This states that when handling stimuli from the environment the brain can deal with only one stimulus at a time. This is because the brain is thought of as a single-channel organ – it can only deal with one piece of information at a time, which has to be processed before the next stimulus can be dealt with. This is often referred to as the 'bottleneck'.

Figure 10.11 Reacting to the gun in a race is an example of simple reaction time

one stimulus and only one possible response, it is known as **simple reaction time**. If there is more than one stimulus and more than one response, then it is called **choice reaction time.**

- The age of the performer – experience speeds up reactions, but age also slows responses down.
- Gender – males tend to have quicker reactions but this degenerates with age more quickly than in females.
- Previous experience – the more experience, the more likely you are to know what to expect and anticipate what to do.
- The number of stimuli to deal with. One stimulus may delay reactions due to the **psychological refractory period.** This is a period of time that it takes for one stimulus to be recognised and cleared before the next stimulus. The delay is caused by the brain being unable to process more than a single item of information at any one time. This theory is called the **single-channel hypothesis.**

In practice

Psychological refractory period

'Selling a dummy' is a typical way of delaying an opponent's tackle. The opponent has to clear the initial decision to tackle before dealing with the realisation that a 'dummy' has taken place. This can give a player valuable time to change direction or make an unexpected pass.

Figure 10.12

10.3 Motor programmes

As we have seen, our brain's functions are often explained by using a computer analogy so that we can understand more clearly the processes that take place when we are learning and performing skills. To continue with this analogy, there is a theory that states that many of the movements we make in sport are so quick and decisive that there cannot be enough time for consideration. The theory is called the **motor programme theory.**

A motor programme can only be stored in the long-term memory store if there has been a considerable amount of previous experience. For example, an experienced basketball player has dribbled the basketball many thousands of times, so dribbling has become almost second nature. This is because a motor programme has been formed in the player's long-term memory that captures all the movements associated with dribbling the basketball. A novice trying to dribble a basketball has to attend to every aspect of the movement but an expert does not have to concentrate so much on the process because it occurs as a flowing and almost natural response.

The motor programme theory is often referred to as **open-loop control** because any feedback that might be available cannot be acted upon because time is so short, therefore there is no feedback loop. For instance, a goalkeeper in football may save the ball, not because of a reflex action but because a previously learned movement is brought into action very quickly and feedback cannot be considered because time is so short.

Figure 10.13

When there is time for feedback to be acted upon **closed-loop control** is involved. The performer receives feedback on the action as it is taking place. For instance, a golfer driving off the tee can sense whether his swing is effective during the action and may act upon the feedback that is received internally to alter his action during the swing. This is why some golfers do not look at where the ball is going – they have 'sensed' the effectiveness of the swing. This internal feedback is often referred to as **proprioception** or **kinaesthesis.** The loop is closed because feedback is present and there is time to modify the movement taking place.

Figure 10.14 Golfers experience internal feedback

Application of the programme theory

If movements can be made quickly in sport there are many advantages – you will have more time to adjust movements if the situation changes and will also be able to attend to other aspects of the environment. For example, a basketball player who is dribbling does not need to concentrate on the actual skill of the dribble, but can look up for a range of passes or shooting opportunities.

For motor programmes to be lodged in the long-term memory, practice is important. Repeat practice, rehearsing the movements over and over again, will ensure that less conscious control is needed when the skill or group of skills have to be performed in the 'real' game situation. The movements are more likely to be remembered if they are meaningful to the performer, so the coach should make practice relevant and show their importance in the competitive game.

By taking note of internal feedback the performer can also train for closed-loop control. If coaching practices are as close to 'real-life' situations as possible, then the internal feedback experienced in training can be more easily acted upon in the high-pressure game situation.

10.4 Principles of skill learning

Motor learning and performance

There is a difference between learning and performance, although often they are treated as if they are the same. **Learning involves a change in behaviour that is relatively permanent**. If you saw a child serve well in tennis once out of 20 attempts, only a limited amount of learning has taken place.

Performance is a *temporary* measurement of learning, but it varies over time, and performance is not a measure of permanent learning. One performance at any particular time is not an accurate measure of learning. Hence the child playing tennis may show one good performance, but looking at their serve over a period of time shows that their learning is limited.

Learning curves

A learning curve is a collection of measurements of performance, and refers to the relationship between practice trials and levels of performance. This relationship is really a curve of performance but the overall picture of performances gives us an idea of the amount of learning that has taken place.

Performances may vary considerably over a period of time and any graph that is constructed showing performances of a newly learned skill over a given time will probably show a learning curve that is not smooth. However, if you took out all the extremes in performances, you would probably find that a curve of sorts would be visible. Obviously the more trials that you record the better indication you will get of the learning that is taking place.

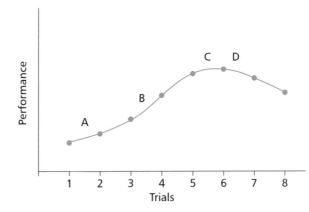

Figure 10.15 Levels of performance over a period of trials

The S-shaped curve shows that there is an initial period when there is no learning. The performer may fail completely in the early stages of learning a motor skill. At position A you can see a slow rate of improvement over the early trials, when the performer is starting to learn the skill. The curve at A is called a **positive acceleration curve** (Honeybourne *et al.*, 2000).

At point B there is a sharp increase in performance levels over a relatively short period of time. The performer seems to be learning quickly now and consequently the performances are rapidly improving. This part of the overall picture is called a **linear curve of learning**, which is not a curve at all but a straight line showing a short period of proportional improvement.

At point C improvements in performances are slowing. This may be because the performer has reached his or her optimum or best possible performances, or could be due to fatigue or lack of motivation to do better. This curve is called a **negative curve of learning**.

The performer then enters a period, shown at point D, where there is no improvement, or even a decrease in performance. This is called the **plateau effect**.

> **Definition**
>
> *Plateau*
>
> Overall there is little or no change in the measured performance. Performances neither increase nor decrease.

Ways to limit the plateau effect
- **Motivation** – vary the practices and use positive feedback.
- **Rest** – to combat physical and/or mental fatigue.
- **Give goals** that are new and challenging but achievable.
- **Give rewards** and praise to encourage.
- **Give physical and mental training** to prepare the performer and to offset the effects of fatigue.

▎*In practice*

When coaching or teaching a novice goal shooting in netball, for instance, be aware that at times improvements could slow, and performance could even get worse – after 20 trials the novice may well be getting fewer goals than after 10 trials. Give the novice a rest and reassess what you are trying to achieve. Go back to technique and give the novice success again to improve confidence. Make the novice aware of the plateau effect and reassure and encourage. Give plenty of praise when it is earned.

Practice principles

Basic to complex

It is common to teach basic skills first and then to build upon these skills to achieve more complex skills.

In primary schools, basic throwing and catching, kicking and striking activities are encouraged so that the basic skills can be transferred to more complex activities such as passing in football and netball or the serve in tennis. Skill teaching is therefore progressive and involves a step-by-step approach from basic 'foundation' actions to more finely tuned complex skills.

To ensure that training practices are helpful, the coach must bear in mind that positive transfer of skills will take place only if they are relevant to the real game situation.

▌▌ *In practice*

A dribbling practice in hockey that uses passive and then gradually more active opposition is going to be far more effective than dribbling around traffic cones!

The amount of positive transfer that can take place depends on how well previously performed skills have been learned. If a skill is broken down and taught in parts, each part must be learned thoroughly before those parts can contribute to the whole skill.

The structure and presentation of practices

For effective skill learning the coach must create the best possible practice conditions. Variety in training is very important, not just to build up experiences in the long-term memory but also to increase interest and motivation.

▌▌ *In practice*

For practice to be meaningful and relevant the following factors need to be taken into consideration:

- *The nature of the skills involved – are they open or closed for instance?*
- *The amount of technical knowledge needed.*
- *The amount of information the performer needs to process.*
- *Environmental factors.*
- *The previous experience of the performer.*
- *The performer's personality and how well they are motivated.*

(adapted from Honeybourne et al., 2000)

*Figure 10.16
Realistic practice is best*

Open skills

These need high levels of information processing and may be broken down into easier sub-routines. As the performer improves skills can be made more complex, until the complete task can be performed.

A highly organised skill

Skills that are difficult to split into sub-routines, often continuous skills such as cycling, should be practised as a whole.

A skill with low organisation

This skill is easily broken down into its constituent parts, for example the tennis serve. The serve involves preparation, throwing up the ball, striking it and finally following through.

▌▌ *In practice*

The highly organised skill of cycling would have to be taught as a whole movement, because of the difficulty of splitting it into sub-routines. The use of stabilisers is common; these enable the novice to experience the action safely and effectively. The novice will eventually be able to cycle without the stabilisers, first with manual support and then without any help.

The low organisation of the tennis serve is best practised by splitting the skill up into its constituent parts. The throwing action of the arm could be practised first, followed by throwing the ball up, hitting it and following through. Eventually the separate actions could be brought together.

(adapted from Honeybourne et al., 2000)

Progressive part method

This is sometimes called **chaining** in the coaching of skills. A serial skill is broken down into its constituent sub-routines, which are thought of as the links of a chain. The performer learns one link at a time, and then adds on a second link. The two links are then practised together, and then a third link is added – and so on, until the links form a chain that can be practised as a whole.

Coaches often employ a mixture of part and whole methods, which can be very effective. First the performer gets the idea of the complete movement and understands the interrelationships between the various components. Each component could then be practised separately to ensure thorough learning. The elements of the skill are then brought together again and performed as a whole.

Massed and distributed practice

Massed practice means practice with very short, or no, rest intervals within the practice session. It is a continuous and intensive period of practice. Massed practice may help in learning discrete skills that are relatively short in duration. A basketball player may use this type of practice for shooting.

Distributed practice involves relatively long rests between sessions. Many performers use the intervals between activities to mentally rehearse their skill performances, which can aid the physical performance later.

Research favours distributed practice because massed practice can hinder learning, mainly because of fatigue and demotivation. Distributed practice is best for continuous skills because the player tires easily. Dangerous tasks, for instance in gymnastics, are better trained for using distributed practice because it ensures that physical and mental fatigue do not interfere with concentration and strength.

Guidance in the teaching of motor skills

There are four main types of guidance in the teaching and coaching of sports skills:

- Visual – e.g. demonstrations (modelling); video playback/analysis.
- Verbal – e.g. instructions; shouting cues.
- Manual – e.g. supporting a gymnastic move.
- Mechanical – e.g. using a twisting belt in trampolining.

The types chosen depend on the personality, motivation and ability of the performer, the situation in which learning or development of skills is taking place, and the nature of the skill being taught or developed (Honeybourne *et al.*, 2000).

Figure 10.17 Visual guidance involves video playback

With visual guidance, it is important that the coach ensures that demonstrations:

- are accurate.
- are repeated but hold the attention and interest of the performer.

With manual or mechanical guidance coaches should bear in mind that manual/mechanical guidance can improve confidence in situations that are perceived to be dangerous (e.g. armbands in learning how to swim).

With verbal guidance the coach should consider:

- that verbal guidance has limitations if used on its own.
- that verbal guidance for the more advanced performer is effective when complex information, such as tactics and strategies, need to be learned.
- attention spans are short in the heat of competitive sport, so the coach should not speak for too long.
- some movements cannot be explained and visual guidance should be used as much as possible.

Questioning techniques encourage participation in learning, which is far more effective than if you are just a passive recipient of information.

Progress check

1 What are the main characteristics associated with someone who is skilful?
2 Give two types of abilities.
3 Explain the main difference between a skill and an ability.
4 What are discrete, serial and continuous skills? Give an example of each.
5 How should you practise a discrete closed skill?
6 Draw a simple flow diagram to show the concept of information processing.
7 What is meant by perception?
8 What is meant by a motor programme?
9 How do we use feedback in skill learning?
10 Give a practical example of when you would use the part method in skills coaching.
11 What is the difference between massed and distributed practice?
12 Name four types of guidance and give some coaching tips on how and when to use them.

11 Research methodology

This chapter covers the necessary information required by the BTEC specifications for writing a research project and investigating quantitative and qualitative research into sport. This chapter will outline the scientific method and methods of investigations. It will take into account the planning, implementation, interpretation and evaluation of a research project. Students will be able to use the information in this chapter to carry out a research project relevant to the BTEC national requirements but it is beyond the scope of this text to go into detail about data analysis and inferential statistics.

Learning objectives

- To outline the scientific method.

- To describe quantitative and qualitative methods of research.

- To explore ethical issues.

- To understand the concept of hypotheses and experimental design.

- To understand different methods of sampling.

- To evaluate outcomes in relation to reliability and validity.

11.1 The scientific method

If research is to be accurate and meaningful then it must be as objective as possible. The study must involve as representative a sample as possible in a variety of situations but in as controlled a manner as possible. These requirements form the basis for a scientific method. This method should:

- Make objective observations.
- Derive testable hypotheses from these observations.
- Use a method to evaluate these hypotheses.
- Publish the methods used and the findings.

It is important that when a research project is carried out the researcher's prejudices are set aside. You should look for this when you evaluate a piece of research.

**Observations → Hypothesis → Testing →
Hypothesis upheld or hypothesis refuted**

Research is crucial if sports performance is to be understood and improved. Different coaching techniques and training regimes may well be introduced as a result of research. For example, the following research questions may produce results that can be used to improve performance:

- Does interval training improve the fitness of rugby players?
- Does carbohydrate loading improve the performance of marathon runners?
- Are visual guidance techniques useful in the acquisition of motor skills?
- Do stress management techniques make athletes less anxious before competition?

11.2 Methods of investigation

Quantitative and qualitative research

Research can be classified into two types: quantitative and qualitative. These two approaches are often combined in research and data that is received can be both quantitative and qualitative.

The quantitative approach

This refers to research that aims to measure the effects of one variable on another as objectively as possible. It involves acquiring data, analysing it and communicating the results. The data gained from this type of research is about 'quantities' of things. The data involves scores, percentages, means and standard deviations – for example, the measurement of the amount of fouls in a game of basketball in games that are close.

The qualitative approach

This refers to the 'qualities' of things. It includes descriptions, meanings and notes about how something is experienced. The researcher is looking at 'what is going on?' rather than 'what is the result?' An example is a training diary of an elite athlete, which may reveal their training habits.

Quasi and non-experimental methods

The investigator using these methods will not manipulate the variables – he or she studies something that would have occurred anyway and has not been affected by the research. In quasi experiments, sometimes called **natural experiments**, a variable has changed but not as a result of the investigation. The advantage of this method is that the setting is natural and 'real life' so there is high **validity,** an important consideration that we will deal with later. The problem with this type of experiment is that variables are difficult to isolate so cause and effect cannot be established.

A non-experimental method is the **observation** approach. This is particularly valuable if research is related to sports psychology, where behaviour is watched and recorded in real-life situations. There are three main types of observational research:

- **Naturalistic observation**, when behaviour is observed in a natural situation.
- **Participant observation**, when the investigator is part of the group being observed.
- **Controlled observation**, when behaviour is observed in a controlled setting.

▌▌▌*In practice*

An example of a participant observer

If an investigator wanted to find out whether being in a particular football supporters' gang led to violence he could pretend that he was a supporter of the team, gain the gang's confidence and then observe their behaviour. The gang members' behaviour would not be affected by being studied if they were not aware of the real intent of the investigator. This can, of course, be an extremely dangerous way of observing behaviour!

Figure 11.1 Participant observation can be dangerous!

Another non-experimental method is called **correlational research**. This is examining a relationship between two variables, for example 'the more of a glucose-rich drink a sports performer drinks, the faster she runs'. There is no manipulation of the variables and if the values of one variable match the values of the other variable this is called a **positive correlation**. If there are low values of one variable but high values of another, then it is known as **a negative correlation**. Note that a negative correlation still illustrates that there is a relationship between the two variables – not that there is no relationship.

▌▌▌*In practice*

Correlation

Positive correlation – the more times an athlete trains, the better his cardiovascular fitness.
Negative correlation – the more alcoholic drinks a gymnast consumes, the less co-ordinated she is. (Don't try this one as a piece of research!)

Case studies are another example of a non-experimental method. This involves investigation in detail of a particular individual, a group of people or an organisation – for instances a case study of an Olympic rower, a case study of a college netball team or a case study of a local-authority sport and leisure department. A case study is very descriptive and is notoriously unscientific, but it gives a very useful and in-depth insight into people or organisations.

The **interview technique** is a very useful way of collecting information; the maximum amount of information can be gained by clever questioning and thoughtful follow-up questions. Interviews can be informal or structured but with both there is a great deal of preparation to be done before the

Figure 11.2 An Olympic rower would make an interesting case study

Independent variable (IV)

The item or items that are changed by the investigator, for example the amount of praise given to a sports performer, affects the level of performance. The IV here is the amount of praise given.

Dependent variable (DV)

The item that is to be measured. The DV in the above example is the level of performance, for example the faster the performer runs.

actual face-to-face interview. Questions can be 'open', allowing for descriptive answers (e.g. 'How do you feel after you lose a game?'), or closed, allowing certain answers only (usually yes or no). An example of a closed question is 'Which team do you play for?'.

Questionnaires and surveys are also methods that are non-experimental. They involve a list of questions, and often but not necessarily large numbers of people. The way a questionnaire is constructed is crucial if the right sort of information is to be gained. If questions are poor then answers may well be biased, with the respondent simply giving the answer he or she thinks they ought to give. The **sample** that is used is important when giving out a questionnaire. It must be representative of the population that you wish the findings to relate to. For example, if you want to find out what athletes think of fartlek training questionnaires should not be given out to footballers! If questionnaires are **piloted** (tried out first and then amended if necessary) they tend to be more effective.

The experimental method

This method establishes a link between **cause** and **effect**: whether one variable affects another. There is a deliberate manipulation of the **independent variable** to measure the effect on the **dependent variable.**

Scientists generally prefer the experimental method because there is greater control in isolating what causes a particular effect. There are two types of experiment:

- Laboratory experiments.
- Field experiments.

Experiments that take place under laboratory conditions are very controlled because interference from the environment and other people is limited, thus enabling the investigator to find out the effects of one particular variable. Laboratory experiments that are useful are those whose results can be **generalised**; that is, applied to 'real' situations. The problems associated with laboratory conditions are that they may not be realistic. For example, a sports performer may behave completely differently in a laboratory than in a real competitive situation.

Field experiments are conducted in a natural setting. The variables cannot be controlled so much but in a field experiment the situation is not so artificial and therefore the findings are more easily generalised.

11.3 Ethical issues related to research

Ensuring that research is ethical is very important to protect all the people involved. It is important to avoid **plagiarism** – copying someone else's work or ideas and pretending that they are your own. When reviewing literature or making conclusions you must not directly copy someone else's work. If you do use other people's ideas you must acknowledge the sources of these ideas, usually in a bibliography. If you need to quote from another source you must acknowledge it and use quotation marks.

When you undertake a piece of research and you have an idea that you wish to prove or disprove, then it is tempting to ignore any facts that disagree with your idea. This is clearly unethical. All data should be made available and referred to so that a balanced conclusion based on all the facts can be made.

Research often involves other people and how you deal with them is important for their and your own protection.

In practice
Guidelines for ethical psychological research
- *Participants should give their **informed consent**. If you use children in research you must obtain the consent of their parents or guardians.*
- *Participants must not be **deceived** about what the research is trying to do. There may be occasions when you withhold information so that the research is valid, but this must be limited.*
- *All participants must be **debriefed**. They must be fully informed after the research has taken place, especially if there was an element of deception in the experiment.*
- *Participants have a right to **withdraw** from the experiment.*
- *No undue **stress** or **anxiety** should be induced by your research.*
- *Results must be kept **confidential**. There must be no reference to the names of the participants or any indication of their identities.*
  (adapted from The British Psychological Society's Ethical Principles 1993)

11.4 Hypotheses and experimental design

A **hypothesis** must be formulated before a piece of research can be carried out. A hypothesis is a prediction or informed guess as to what is likely to be discovered. This prediction can then be tested by research to see whether it is correct or incorrect. A hypothesis must be capable of being disproved as well as proved to be testable. There are therefore two hypotheses: the **null hypothesis** and the **experimental hypothesis**.

A statistical test is actually testing the null hypothesis. Is the result due to chance or as a result of the effects of the independent variable? If the statistics show that it is not due to chance then we can reject the null hypothesis and accept the experimental hypothesis.

One- and two-tailed hypotheses

If the experimental hypothesis predicts what the direction of the result is going to be then it is called a **one-tailed hypothesis** (e.g. performance in endurance races in the morning is significantly better than afternoon races). It is called one-tailed because the results are predicted to be towards one end of the distribution of scores.

If the experimental hypothesis does not state the direction of the result then it is called a **two-tailed hypothesis**. For example, 'there will be a significant difference between performances in endurance races in the morning and afternoon'. It is called two-tailed because the predicted result could be at either end of the distribution of scores.

Experimental design

There are three most common designs of experiment.

Independent subjects

The two or more groups used in the experiment consist of different individuals. For instance, a group of boys is compared with a group of girls on the multi-stage fitness test.

- **Advantage**: In this design you can use the same materials and there is no need for a gap between the tests because of fatigue factor.
- **Disadvantage**: Individuals may vary in important characteristics such as previous experience.

Repeated measures

The same individuals are tested in two or more separate 'conditions' (tasks). For example, a group of girls is tested on the multi-stage fitness test, then on a sit-up test and then on a sprint test (always the same girls).

- **Advantage**: There are no subject variables, because the individuals remain the same.
- **Disadvantage**: Doing the first task may affect the next task. This is called **order effects**.

Matched pairs

Different individuals are used in the conditions but they are carefully 'matched' on important factors such as age or height.

Definition

Null hypothesis

This states that any difference or relationship between the independent variable and the dependent variable is only due to chance. For example, 'any difference between the intake of vitamin C tablets and improvement in a cycling sprint is due to chance'.

Experimental hypothesis

This states that there is a significant difference or relationship between the two variables. The word **significant** is important if you use inferential statistics. The experimental hypothesis is accepted as significant if the probability that it is only due to chance is 5% or less. An example is 'there will be a significant difference between the performance of a cycle sprint in those that take vitamin C and those who do not'.

- **Advantage**: There are no order effects and no need to wait between tests.
- **Disadvantage**: It is a time-consuming and complex process and you cannot control all the possible variables between individuals.

Single subject

This is when only one participant is involved in the experiment.
- **Advantage**: In-depth analysis; e.g. case study.
- **Disadvantage**: Difficult to generalise from one subject to lots of others.

11.5 Sampling

If there are individuals or groups involved in the research, then it is important that a sample is selected for our research.
- The **target population** is firstly identified – for example, do you want to test the motor skills of boys and compare them with girls? If so then the target population might be all boys and girls under the age of 11.
- Once the target population has been identified then a group or **sample** must be selected. The sample must be as unbiased and as representative as possible. There are several ways of selecting a sample.

Random sample

This is an extremely valid method to use. Every member of the target population has an equal chance of being selected for the sample. Each member of the target population could be assigned a number, for instance, and the numbers pulled out of a hat to identify the sample. This could be very time consuming if the target population is big. No one member of the target population has a greater chance of being selected than another.

Systematic sampling

Every fifth, tenth, eightieth person in a list of the target population is selected, for instance.

Stratified sampling

In this method each variable affecting the target population is represented. For example, there would be 50% girls in your sample because there are 50% girls in the target population. If 30% of the target population trained in the evening 30% of your sample should be those that trained in the evening.

Opportunity sampling

This sample is selected because they are immediately available. If you wished to select a group of football players, then you would use the local club because they happen to be close by and willing to participate. This type of sampling can cause bias because it is not representative of the target population. For instance, the local football club players may be 100% white and predominantly left footed.

11.6 Reliability and validity

Any research to be considered as serious and meaningful must be consistent and show that it is measuring what it is supposed to measure. For coaches and sports performers to take note of research findings and alter their practice, they must be confident that the research is both **reliable** and **valid**.

Reliability

This refers to the **consistency** of the testing involved. A reliable measure would be one that produces the same results on different occasions. A piece of research into plyometric training, for instance, may show its usefulness to increase power – but if the research was repeated and showed that plyometrics had no effect on power, then the research is not reliable.

An example of measuring reliability is the **test–retest measure**. In this measure the same group of individuals who are given the same test twice will come up with very similar results.

Validity

Validity refers to whether a test measures what it is supposed to measure. A test could be reliable but not valid. For instance, two netball players could be weighed and found to be the same weight (reliable) but this would not indicate that one was a better player than the other (validity).

Some tests in sport may not be particularly valid. A fitness test related to flexibility, for example, may show consistent scores for an individual but it does not measure power, strength or endurance and so it is not a valid test for overall fitness.

Ensuring that your research is valid
- Make sure that your method of measurement is valid.
- Using different types of measurement may increase the validity of your research.
- Questionnaires must not involve bias and questions should be carefully phrased.
- Observations must be carried out as objectively as possible to avoid observer bias.
- Limit **demand characteristics**.
- Avoid experimenter bias by being as detached as possible from the experiment. The experimenter may affect the results.
- Ensure that the research is **ecologically valid**.
- Ensure that the research is not too **ethnocentric**.

11.7 Recommended sources (Edexcel) for information on data analysis

Bernstein, S. and Bernstein, R. *Schaum's Outline of Theory and Problems of Elements of Statistics: Descriptive Statistics and Probability*. McGraw-Hill, 1998.

Bryman, A. and Cramer, D. *Quantitative Data Analysis for Social Scientists*. Routledge, 1999.

Definition

Ecological validity

This means that research must be applicable to 'real life'. In laboratory conditions for instance a sports performer may behave very differently from in a competitive situation. A participant may fill in a questionnaire about anxiety that he or she feels in competition but in the quiet peaceful surroundings of a laboratory. Clearly the answers written on the questionnaire are likely be different from those given when the participant is about to perform in a highly charged atmosphere.

An experiment is ecologically valid if it is as close to real-life conditions as possible.

Definition

Demand characteristics

Participants may try to impose their interpretation on a particular situation. They may guess what the experiment is about and try to conform to the expected outcomes or try to ruin it! A well-designed experiment will minimise these effects.

Definition

Ethnocentricity

The tendency to see things from the point of view of your group and to devalue people that are not in your group. Most sports psychology research, for instance, is done on white American males. It is therefore important not to generalise your findings to the populations that do not have a predominance of white American males! It is important in research to take into account different cultures and groups before it can be generalised.

Burns, R.B. *Introduction to Research Methods*. Sage Publications, 2000.

Flick, U. *An Introduction to Qualitative Research*. Sage Publications, 1998.

Hogg, R.V. and Craig, A.T. *Introduction to Mathematical Statistics*. Prentice Hall, 1994.

Howitt, D. and Cramer, D. *An Introduction to Statistics in Psychology*. Prentice Hall, 2000.

Moore, D.S. and McCabe, G.P. *Introduction to the Practice of Statistics*. W.H. Freeman, 1998.

Nolan, B. *Data Analysis: An Introduction*. Cambridge, 1994.

Ott, L.R. and Longnecker, M. *An Introduction to Statistical Methods and Data Analysis*. Duxbury, 2001.

Punch, K.F. *Introduction to Social Research*. Sage Publications, 1998.

Rice, J.A. *Mathematical Statistics and Data Analysis*. Wadsworth, 1995.

Rohatgi, V.K. *An Introduction to Probability and Statistics*. Wiley, 2000.

Progress check

1. Draw a flow diagram to represent the 'scientific method' of research.
2. What is the difference between quantitative and qualitative research?
3. Give an example of participant-observation research related to sport.
4. (a) What is a positive correlation?
   (b) Give a possible example from sport.
5. What is the advantage of a case study approach?
6. Give one example of an open question and one closed question that you might use in an interview related to sports research.
7. Using an example of a research question related to sport, identify the independent and the dependent variables.
8. Identify four ethical considerations for research.
9. What is the difference between an experimental and a null hypothesis?
10. Give an example of a one-tailed hypothesis and a two-tailed hypothesis that could be used in sports-related research.
11. Outline the repeated-measures research design.
12. What type of sampling is best? Explain your answer.
13. Define reliability and validity.
14. Give an example of a piece of sports-related research that would not be valid. State reasons for your selection.

Appendix

The reflective practitioner

This unit is based upon a student's ability to look at the factors and reasons behind their own, or another person's, sporting performance, and as such has to be approached on an individual basis.

To achieve this analysis, a number of skills are used and developed. These include planning and communication; how they are used and the effects that they have. These combined will allow the student to think about and assess the different elements that affect personal development, planning and sports performance.

Within 'The reflective practitioner', you need to consider the types of communication – personal, intrapersonal and technical – and how these can be used to their best advantage to progress both as a practitioner and as a student. By looking at the methods of communication available to you this will aid the planning context of the unit. Here it is possible to implement what is known as SMART objectives. These are goals that are specific, measurable, achievable, realistic and timed targets.

By studying ways in which you can communicate and plan the SMART objectives, this will help in the preparation of an analysis of a performance and define ways in which the performer can extend their own goals to meet new demands and challenges. Within this structure you will also be able to look at the potential obstacles – barriers to achievement – that could be encountered, and the way in which you could make plans to help overcome these hurdles.

As an internally assessed unit you have the opportunity to carry out the following tasks:

- assess current performance in a chosen sport
- explore targets for future performance in a chosen sport
- produce an effective performance plan taking account of barriers to achievement
- monitor and evaluate performance.

Assessment of current performance

Factors which you need to take account of are:

- Previous experience – what level have you reached in your sport?
- Technical knowledge and skills – what do you know about your sport and what skills have you mastered?
- Technical ability – what underlying abilities do you have?
- Levels of fitness – what test results have you had related to all aspects of your fitness e.g. cardio-vascular / flexibility?
- Commitment, training attendance and effort – how much time and effort do you give to your sport – how many times a week do you train and for how long – do you keep a training diary?

- Access to equipment and facilities – do you have your own equipment for your sport? What facilities do you use? How easy is it to access training equipment and facilities?
- Access to effective coaching – who coaches you? How is this funded? How many coaches do you have?
- Diet – do you keep a food diary? Are there any foods you have to avoid? Does your diet vary depending on the stage of the season or leading up to a competition/match?
- Areas for improvement – having taken into account all of the above, what improvements could be made to enable you to be more effective in your sport?
- Methods of assessment – how do you assess your current performance/ preparation in your sport? Do you use the assessments of others? Do you use video analysis or a coach's match analysis? Do you use a SWOT analysis (strengths; weaknesses; opportunities; threats)? Do you use objective tests such as a recognised fitness test or a psychometric test?

Targets for future performance

- Targets should be based on the SMART principle.
- Targets should be divided into short, medium and long term and seasonal.

Performance plan

Should involve:

- Aims and objectives
- Recognition of resources required
- Set and agreed goals
- Training details and competitions
- Diet details
- Use of any technical equipment
- Recognition of the barriers that need to be overcome. For example:
  - Injury and illness
  - Weather
  - Travel and travel costs
  - Team selection
  - Lack of equipment / facilities
  - Lack of coaching expertise
  - Financial implications to live and train
  - The expectations and demands of others e.g. personal relationships/family.

Monitor and evaluate performance

- Assess performance against SMART targets
- Peer and teacher assessments
- Feedback form coaches and training results
- Acquisition of new skills
- Recommendations for future plans / aims
- Identify support needed, for example training courses, NVQ's or other qualifications.

Selected references and further reading

Allport, G. W. *Attitudes*. Clarke University Press, 1935.

Bandura, A. *Social Learning Theory*. Prentice Hall, 1977.

Baron, R.A. *Human Aggression*. Plenum, 1977.

Barrow, J.L. The variables of leadership. *Academy of Management Review*, 1977.

Berkowitz, L. Some determinants of impulsive aggression. *Psychological Review*, 1974.

Bernstein, S. and Bernstein, R. *Schaum's Outline of Theory and Problems of Elements of Statistics: Descriptive Statistics and Probability*. McGraw-Hill, 1998.

Bryman, A. and Cramer, D. *Quantitative Data Analysis for Social Scientists*. Routledge, 1999.

Bull, S.J. *Sport Psychology, A Self Help Guide*. Crowood, 1991.

Burns, R.B. *Introduction to Research Methods*. Sage Publications, 2000.

Carron, A.V. *Social Psychology of Sport*. Mouvement Publications, 1980.

Chelladurai, P. Multidimensional model of leadership 1984. In: J.M. Silva and R.S. Weinberg, eds. *Psychological Foundations of Sport*. Human Kinetics, 1984.

Coon, D. *Introduction to Psychology*. West Publishing Co., 1983.

Cottrell, N.B. *Performance in the Presence of Other Human Beings*. Allyn & Bacon, 1968.

Cox, R.H. *Sport Psychology Concepts and Applications*. McGraw-Hill, 1998.

Cratty, B.J. *Social Psychology in Athletics*. Prentice Hall, 1981.

Csikszentmihalyi, M. *Beyond Boredom and Anxiety*. Jossey-Bass, 1975.

Davis, D., Kimmet, T. and Auty, M. *Physical Education: Theory and Practice*. Macmillan, 1986.

Deci, F.L. *Intrinsic Motivation and Self-determination in Human Behaviour*. Plenum Press, 1985.

Dollard, J. *Frustration and Aggression*. Yale University Press, 1939.

Duda, J.L. The relationship between task and ego orientation. *Journal of Sports Psychology*, 1989.

Dweck, C.S. *Learned Helplessness in Sport*. Human Kinetics, 1980.

Eysenck, H.J. *The Structure and Measurement of Personality*. Routledge, 1969, 1970.

Festinger, L.A. *A Theory of Cognitive Dissonance*. Harper & Row, 1957.

Festinger, L. *Social Pressures in Informal Groups*. Harper & Row, 1963.

Fiedler, F.E. *A Theory of Leadership Effectiveness*. McGraw-Hill, 1967.

Fitts, P.M. *Human Performance*. Brooks/Cole, 1967.

Flick, U. *An Introduction to Qualitative Research*. Sage Publications, 1998.

Gill, D.L. *Psychological Dynamics of Sport*. Human Kinetics, 1986.

Gill, D.L. and Deeter, T.E. Development of the Sport Orientation Questionnaire. *Research Quarterly for Sport*, 1988.

Hinkle, J.S. *et al*. Running behaviour. *Journal of Sport Behaviour*, 15, 1989, pp. 263–277.

Hogg, R.V. and Craig, A.T. *Introduction to Mathematical Statistics*. Prentice Hall, 1994.

Hollander, E.R. *Principles and Methods of Social Psychology*, 2nd edition. Oxford University Press, 1971.

Honeybourne, J., Hill, M. and Moors, H. *Advanced Physical Education and Sport for A-level*, 2nd edition. Nelson Thornes, 2000.

Honeybourne, J., Hill, M. and Wyse. J. *PE for You*. Stanley Thornes, 1998.

Howitt, D. and Cramer, D. *An Introduction to Statistics in Psychology*. PrenticeHall, 2000.

Hull, C.L. *Principles of Behaviour*. Appleton-Century-Crofts, 1943.

Ingham, A.G. *et al*. The Ringelmann effect. *Journal of Experimental Psychology*, 1974.

Jarvis, M. *Sports Psychology*. Routledge, 1999.

Jones, J.G. and Hardy, L. (eds) *Stress and Performance in Sport*. Wiley, 1990.

Knapp, B. *Skills in Sport*. Routledge, 1965.

Kroll, W. *et al*. Multivariate personality profile analysis of four athletic groups. In: R. Cox, *Sports Pychology*. WCB/McGraw-Hill, 1998.

Latane, B. *et al*. Many hands make light work. *Journal of Personality*, 1979.

Levitt, E.E. *The Psychology of Anxiety*. Erlbaum, 1980.

Lewin, K. *A Dynamic Theory of Personality*. McGraw-Hill, 1935.

Lewin, K. *Psychological Theory*. Macmillan, 1951.

Locke, E.A. and Latham, G.P. The application of goal setting in sports. *Journal of Sports Psychology*, 7, 1985, pp. 205–222.

Lorenz, K. *On Aggression*. Brace & World, 1966.

Magill, R.A. *Motor Learning, Concepts and Applications*. Brown and Benchmark, 1993.

Martens, R. Science and sport psychology. *The Sports Psychologist*, 1987.

Martens, R., Vealey, R.S. and Burton D. *Competitive Anxiety in Sport*. Human Kinetics, 1990.

Moore, D.S. and McCabe, G.P. *Introduction to the Practice of Statistics*. W.H. Freeman, 1998.

Morgan, W.P. *Sport Personology*. Mouvement, 1980.

Mosston, M. and Ashworth, S. *Teaching Physical Education*. Merrill, 1986.

Nolan, B. *Data Analysis: An Introduction*. Cambridge University Press, 1994.

Ott, L.R. and Longnecker, M. *An Introduction to Statistical Methods and Data Analysis*. Duxbury, 2001.

Pervin, L. *Personality Theory and Research*. Wiley, 1993.

Punch, K.F. *Introduction to Social Research*. Sage Publications, 1998.

Radford, J. and Govier, E. (eds) *A Textbook of Psychology*. Routledge, 1991.

Rice, J.A. *Mathematical Statistics and Data Analysis*. Wadsworth, 1995.

Robb, M. *The Dynamics of Skill Acquisition*. Prentice Hall, 1972.

Roberts, C.G., Spink, K.S. and Pemberton, C.L. *Learning Experiences in Sport Psychology*. Human Kinetics, 1986.

Roberts, K.C. and Pascuzzi, D. Causal attributions in sport. *Journal of Sports Psychology*, 1979.

Roberts, G.C. (ed.) *Motivation in Sport and Exercise*. Human Kinetics, 1992.

Rohatgi, V.K. *An Introduction to Probability and Statistics*. Wiley, 2000.

Sage, G.H. *Sport and American Society*. Addison-Wesley, 1974.

Schmidt, R.A. *Motor Learning and Performance*. Human Kinetics, 1991.

Schurr, K.T. *et al*. A multivariate analysis of athletic characteristics. *Multivariate Experimental Clinical Research*, 3, 1977, pp. 53–68.

Sharp, R. *Acquiring Skill in Sport*. Sports Dynamics, 1992.

Shaw, M.E. *Group Dynamics*. McGraw-Hill, 1976.

Silva, J.M. and Weinberg, R.S. (eds) *Psychological Foundations of Sport*. Human Kinetics, 1984.

Skinner, B.F. *Science and Human Behaviour*. Macmillan, 1953.

Smoll, F.L. and Shutz, R.W. Children's attitudes towards physical activity. *Journal of Sports Psychology*, 1980.

Steiner, I.D. *Group Process and Productivity*. Academic Press, 1972.

Thorndike, E.L. *Educational Psychology: Briefer Course*. Columbia University Press, 1914.

Triandis, H.C. *Interpersonal Behaviour*. Brooks/Cole, 1977.

Weinberg, R.S. The relationship between extrinsic rewards and intrinsic motivation. In: J.M. Silva and R.S. Weinberg (eds) *Psychological Foundations of Sport*. Human Kinetics, 1984.

Wesson K. *et al*. *Sport and P.E.* Hodder and Stoughton, 1998.

Willis, J.D. and Campbell, L.F. *Exercise Psychology*. Human Kinetics, 1992.

Wood, B. *Applying Psychology to Sport*. Hodder & Stoughton, 1998.

Yerkes, R.M. and Dodson, J. D. The relation of strength of stimulus to rapidity of habit formation. *Journal of Neurological Psychology*, 1908.

Glossary

All or none law   The strength of the stimulus is important in muscle contraction – if it is strong enough to activate at least one motor unit then *all* the fibres within that unit will contract. Neurones and muscle fibres either respond completely – all – or not at all – none.

Amino acids   These are the building blocks of proteins. There are ten amino acids that we are unable to make for ourselves: these are called essential amino acids. Examples are leucine and threonine. We have to take in the essential amino acids as part of our diet. The other twelve amino acids are called non-essential, because we can manufacture them. Examples are glycine and glutamine.

Anatomical position   This refers to a person standing upright, facing forwards, arms hanging downward, with the palms of the hands facing forward.

Antioxidant vitamins   These are beta carotene, vitamin C and vitamin E (sometimes known as the ACE vitamins). They can help prevent damage to muscles and reduce post-exercise muscle soreness.

Anxiety   'A negative emotional state caused by a situation that is seen as threatening.' – Woods 1998.
   'Subjective feeling of apprehension and heightened physiological arousal.' – Levitt 1980.

Arousal   A term used for the intensity of the drive that is experienced by an athlete when trying to achieve a goal. High arousal can lead to high levels of stress, both physiological and psychological.

Cancellous bone   This is often called spongy bone and has a honeycomb appearance, which provides a strong structure that is very light. It consists of bone tissue called trabeculae, which is connective tissue, with red bone marrow.

Cardiovascular   Cardio – means heart. Vascular – circulatory networks of the blood vessels.

Cholesterol   This is a type of fat that is actually essential to a healthy life. It is produced by the liver and taken in in the diet. Cholesterol is carried around the body in the blood attached to lipoproteins, which come in two forms – 'good' LDL (low-density lipoprotein) and 'bad' HDL (high-density lipoprotein). HDL carrying cholesterol is 'bad' because it causes the accumulation of cholesterol in the vessel walls; the 'good' LDL transports the cholesterol back to the liver for disposal.

Cognitive skills   Skills that involve intellectual ability. These skills affect the perceptual process and help us to make sense of what is required in any given situation. They are essential if the performer is to make correct and effective decisions.

Compact bone   This hard bone forms the surface layers of all bones. It helps to protect bones and is surrounded by the periosteum, which is a fibrous, vascular tissue containing blood vessels.

Competitive Trait Anxiety   'A tendency to perceive competitive situations as threatening and to respond to these situations with feelings of apprehension or tension.' – Martens 1977.

Demand characteristics   Participants may try to impose their interpretation on a particular situation. They may guess what the experiment is about and try to conform to the expected outcomes or try to ruin it! A well-designed experiment will minimise these effects.

Dependent variable (DV)   The item that is to be measured. The DV in the above example is the level of performance, for example the faster the performer runs.

Diabetes   Diabetes is caused by a complete lack of insulin or a reduction of insulin production in the body. The hormone insulin, produced by the pancreas is used to control blood glucose. With little or no insulin to trigger the breakdown of sugar, the cells cannot use glucose. There is consequently a rise in blood sugar, which becomes dangerous if not treated.

Ecological validity   This means that research must be applicable to 'real life'. In laboratory conditions for instance a sports performer may behave very differently than in a competitive situation. A participant may fill in a questionnaire about anxiety that he or she feels in competition but in the quiet peaceful surroundings of a laboratory. Clearly the answers written on the questionnaire are likely be different from those given when the participant is about to perform in a highly charged atmosphere. An experiment is ecologically valid if it is as close to real life conditions as possible.

Ethnocentricity   The tendency to see things from the point of view of your group and to devalue people that are not in your group. Most sports psychology research, for instance, is done on White American males. It is therefore important not to generalise your findings to the populations that do not have a predominance of White American males! It is important in research to take into account different cultures and groups before it can be generalised.

Experimental hypothesis   This states that there is a significant difference or relationship between the two variables. The word significant is important if you use inferential statistics. The experimental hypothesis is accepted as significant if the probability that is only due to chance is 5% or less. An example is 'there will be a significant difference between the performance of a cycle sprint in those that take vitamin C and those who do not.'

Extravert   Seeks social situations and likes excitement. Lacks concentration.

Extrinsic motivation   The drive that is caused by motives that are external or environmental. These motives are rewards that can be tangible or intangible.

FITT   F   Frequency of training (number of training sessions each week).
        I   Intensity of the exercise undertaken.
        T   Time or duration that the training takes up.
        T   Type of training to be considered that fulfils specific needs.

Fundamental motor skills   Very basic skills like jumping, kicking and throwing. We learn these skills at a young age, usually through play. If these fundamental motor skills are learned thoroughly, we can build the more complex actions required in sport upon them.

Gross motor ability   Ability involving actual movement – for example, strength, flexibility, speed.

Group   A collection of individuals who share similar goals and who interact.
    'A group is defined as two or more persons who are interacting with one another in such a manner that each person influences and is influenced by each other person.' – Shaw 1976.
    'A collective identity, a sense of shared purpose or objectives, structured patterns of interaction, structured modes of communication. personal and/or task interdependence and interpersonal attraction.' – Carron 1980.

Haemoglobin   This is an iron-rich protein, which transports the oxygen in the blood. The more haemoglobin there is in an erythrocyte, the more oxygen it can carry. This concentration can be increased through endurance training.

Hazard   Something that has the potential to cause harm.

Hick's Law   This states that: 'Choice reaction time is linearly related to the amount of information that must be processed to resolve the uncertainty about the various possible stimulus response alternatives.' In other words, the more alternatives, the longer your reaction time.

Independent variable (IV)   The item or items that are changed by the investigator, for example the amount of praise given to a sports performer affects the level of performance. The IV here is the amount of praise given.

Insertion   This is the end of the muscle that is attached to the bone that moves. For example, the insertion of the biceps is on the radius, which moves when the muscle contracts.

Intrinsic motivation   'Inner striving to be competent and self-determining; a sense of mastery over a task and to feel a sense of achievement' – Martens 1987.

Introvert   Does not seek social situations, likes peace and quiet. Good at concentrating.

Karnoven Principle   This formula identifies correct training intensities as a percentage of the sum of the maximum heart rate reserve and resting heart rate. It is a valid measure because it takes into account the stress on the heart and the percentage of VO_2 max of the athlete. The maximum heart rate reserve is calculated by subtracting an individual's resting heart rate from their maximum heart rate. The maximum heart rate can be calculated by subtracting age from 220. It is suggested that the average athlete should work at a training intensity of 60–75% of maximal heart rate reserve.

Kinaesthetic sense   This is the feeling or sense that we get through movement. Our proprioceptors (found in our muscles, ligament and joints) pick up signals that feed back to the brain to tell us where we are and what we are doing. For example, the kinaesthetic sense of cycling with stabilisers will be different to the feelings that you get from muscles when you are cycling without mechanical help. Therefore it is important to get the 'true' sense of the skill as quickly as you can in skill learning.

Leadership   'The behavioural process influencing individuals and groups towards set goals.' – Barrow 1977.

Learned helplessness   This is a psychological phenomenon that arises from failure on a task or tasks that has been reinforced. There is then avoidance behaviour with that task or tasks. 'I was hopeless at sport at school, it is no good me trying sport again – I will only fail.'

Learning   'The more or less permanent change in behaviour that is reflected in a change in performance.' – Knapp 1965.
  'A relatively permanent change in behaviour due to past experience.' – Coon 1983.

Mob football   This was a mass game with very few rules which was played occasionally in or between villages. The game was a football/rugby type game and was often extremely violent.

Motivation   'A drive to fulfil a need.' – Gill 1986.
  'Energization and direction of behaviour.' – Roberts 1992.
  'The internal mechanisms and external stimuli, which arouse and direct our behaviour.' – Sage 1977.

Motor programme   A generalised series of movements, stored in the long-term memory and triggered by making one decision.

Motor skill   An action or task that has a goal and which requires voluntary body and/or limb movement to achieve the goal.

Movement time   The time between starting and finishing a movement. The sprinter drives off the blocks, and begins running.

Need to achieve (Nach)   This is a personality type that involves the following characteristics:

- They persist on task.
- They complete the task quickly.
- They take risks.
- They take personal responsibility for their actions.
- They like feedback about their performance.

Need to avoid failure (Naf)   People with a Naf personality have the following characteristics:

- They give up on tasks easily.
- They take their time to complete the task.
- They avoid challenging situations.
- They do not take personal responsibility for their actions.
- They do not want feedback about results or performance.

Neurotic   Highly anxious and has unpredictable emotions.

Null hypothesis   This states that any difference or relationship between the independent variable and the dependent variable is only due to chance. For example, 'any difference between the intake of vitamin C tablets and improvement in a cycling sprint is due to chance'.

Origin   The end of the muscle attached to a bone that is stationary, e.g. the scapula. The origin remains still when contraction occurs. Some muscles have two or more origins, e.g. the biceps has two heads, which pull on the one insertion to lift the lower arm.

Personality   'The sum total of an individual's characteristics that make him unique' – Hollander 1971.

'Personality represents those characteristics of the person that account for consistent patterns of behaviour' – Pervin 1993.

'The more or less stable and enduring organisation of a person's character, temperament, intellect and physique which determines the unique adjustment to the environment' – Eysenck 1960.

'Personality is an overall pattern of psychological characteristics that makes each person a unique individual' – Gill 1986.

Plateau   Overall there is little or no change in the measured performance. Performances neither increase nor decrease.

Psychomotor ability   The ability to process information regarding movement and then to put decisions into action. Psychomotor abilities include reaction time and limb co-ordination.

QUEST   The scheme, with origins in the British Quality Association Leisure Services Sub Committee, was launched in 1996, to set clear standards and encourage continuous improvement in sport and leisure activities.

Reaction time   The time between first presentation of a stimulus to the very start of the movement in response to it. For example, a sprinter hears the gun and decides to drive off the blocks (no movement yet).

Response time   The time between first presentation of a stimulus to completion of the movement (reaction time plus movement time) – in this example from the time the sprinter first hears the gun to reaching full sprint.

Risk   The chance that someone will be harmed by a hazard.

Risk assessment   The technique by which you measure up the chances of an accident happening, anticipate what the consequences would be and plan what actions to prevent it.

Saturated fats These are usually solid (e.g. lard) and primarily from animal sources.

Single-channel hypothesis   This states that when handling stimuli from the environment the brain can deal with only one stimulus at a time. This is because the brain is thought of as a single-channel organ – it can only deal with one piece of information at a time, which has to be processed before the next stimulus can be dealt with. This is often referred to as the 'bottleneck'.

Sliding filament theory   This theory was put forward by Huxley in 1969 to explain how a muscle alters its length. When a muscle contracts:

- the I band shortens
- the A band remains the same length
- the H band disappears.

The myosin pulls the actin across so that the two filaments slide closer together, but the filaments do not actually get any shorter.

Socialisation   This is a process of adopting the norms and values of your culture. It is about learning to be an accepted citizen. Appropriate behaviour is normally learned in the formative years from significant others such as parents.

Social learning   The influences of others on a person's behaviour. We observe and imitate role models but only those who are significant to us.

Sports equity   'This is concerned with fairness in sport, equality of access, recognizing inequalities and taking steps to address them. It is about changing the culture and structure of sport to ensure that it becomes equally accessible to all members of society, whatever their age, ability, gender, race, ethnicity, sexuality or social/economic status. Sports equity, then, is more concerned with the sport itself.' – Sport England 2002.

SPRITO   This is the national training organisation for sport, recreation and allied occupations. It includes training for leisure attractions, health and fitness, the outdoors, the caravan industry, playwork and sport and recreation.

Stable   Does not swing from one emotion to another.

State anxiety (A State)   This is the anxiety in a particular situation. There are two types of state anxiety :

- Somatic – the body's response e.g. tension, rapid pulse rate.
- Cognitive – the psychological worry over the situation.

Stress   'Stress is a pattern of negative physiological states and psychological responses occurring in situations where people perceive threats to their well being which they may be unable to meet.' – Lazarus and Folkman 1984.
   '. . . process whereby an individual perceives a threat and responds with a series of psychological and physiological changes including increased arousal and the experience of anxiety.' – Jarvis 1999.

Team cohesion   Cohesion concerns the motivational aspects, which attract individual members to the group and the resistance of those members to the group breaking up.' – Honeybourne *et al.*, 2000.
   'The total field of forces, which act on members to remain in the group.' – Festinger et al 1963.

Trait anxiety (A Trait)   This is a personality trait that is enduring in the individual. A performer with high trait anxiety has the predisposition or the potential to react to situations with apprehension.

Unsaturated fats   These are usually liquid (e.g. vegetable oil) and come from plant sources.

Vasoconstriction   This occurs when the artery walls contract and the diameter of the artery decreases. The vessels can therefore help to change the pressure of the blood, which is especially important during exercise.

Vasodilation   This occurs when the artery walls relax and the diameter of the artery increases.

Index